West Academic Publishing's Law School Advisory Board

Legal Writing

Deborah L. Borman
Professor of Law
University of Arkansas Little Rock
William H. Bowen School of Law

A SHORT & HAPPY GUIDE® SERIES

WEST
ACADEMIC
PUBLISHING

a short & happy guide series is a trademark registered in the U.S. Patent and Trademark Office.

© 2019 LEG, Inc. d/b/a West Academic

    444 Cedar Street, Suite 700
    St. Paul, MN 55101
    1-877-888-1330

Printed in the United States of America

ISBN: 978-1-63459-918-4

Acknowledgments

This short book was long in the making. The lion's share of my gratitude goes to my former students, teaching assistants, and research assistants, from to Chicago to Seattle, all who contributed ideas, humorous anecdotes, advice, creativity, and time in the interest of educating law students and future attorneys: Saloni Shah, Victoria Banks, Jonathan Kirschmeier, and Shareen Sarwar. Additionally, I thank Rachel Mika for her attention to detail, Karin Mika for being my Catcher in the Rye, LeighAnne Thompson for contributions both earthly and metaphysical, and Dianna Cramer for advice and artistic expertise. I could never do what I do without the support of my numerous friends and professor colleagues around the country; you are my family and I love you all. Finally, thanks to my editors at West for their extreme patience.

I dedicate this book to the memory of my dad who would ask: "Where are your illustrations?"

Next time, dad. I promise.

About the Author

Deborah L. Borman is a Professor at the University of Arkansas Little Rock William H. Bowen School of Law. Prior to her current appointment, Professor Borman taught legal analysis and advocacy courses at Northwestern, DePaul, and John Marshall in Chicago, and at Seattle University and the University of Denver. A citizen of the world, she considers Chicago her heart home.

Table of Contents

PART III. HAPPY WRITING STRUCTURE

PART IV. HAPPY PERSUASIVE BRIEFS

PART V. LEGAL WRITING QUICK TIPS

A Short & Happy Guide to Legal Writing

Introduction

Lawyers have a reputation for excellent written communication. We excel at storytelling and persuasion and are experts at using these arts to win disputes (and to mitigate damages). Writing is the specialized tool of the successful attorney in storytelling, persuasion, and winning (and mitigation); specialized because we are trained to think through the resolution of legal issues and to express our analyses in writing.

Despite the importance and excellence of writing in law practice, or maybe because of it, legal writing is without a doubt the most feared course prior to, and during the first year of law school. Students are intimidated by the prospect of writing, let alone legal writing, and bring a variety of pre-conceived notions about themselves, the writing course, and their abilities to the legal writing classroom.

Welcome to the Short & Happy Guide to Legal Writing. This book will dispel the notion that legal writing is awful or terrible and alleviate your fears about legal writing. Legal writing is not so much *writing,* as the expression into writing of the thoughtful legal analysis that you construct to resolve a legal problem. The process of putting legal analysis into writing is not difficult! Did you just read what I wrote and balk? Do you doubt me? Let me say that again: *the process of putting legal analysis into writing is not difficult.*

The process of constructing a legal analysis, which not difficult *per se*, does involve a commitment to learning, self-training, and practice to cultivate your mind to think about form and content of writing in entirely new directions. The legal writing learning process, therefore, demands time, energy, and commitment. By time, energy, and commitment, I do not mean purely time-consuming, however. Consumption of time has an understood negative connotation. Instead what I am telling you is that if you give yourself the proper time and space to learn the framework for legal analysis, to practice the art of constructing a legal analysis, to teach yourself to think, and to test yourself on your process through practice, you will possess a skill that you will have for life and that can never be taken away from you: the productive, legal-analytical mind.

In this book, I will introduce you both to the form and substance of legal writing. I will provide a framework that you will use construct your legal analyses for law school, and probably every other analysis you will construct throughout your legal career.

There are no real tricks or shortcuts to constructing a legal analysis, but over time you will become so proficient at using the framework, that constructing your analysis within this framework will become second nature.

You will likely have many other resources and required readings for your writing class with many samples to work with; use those resources to the limits. My goal is that this book will help you streamline your writing process and that you will have a little fun along the way.

One of the basic skills a lawyer must have is the ability to think like a lawyer. This might seem self-evident, but thinking like a lawyer is something that takes some time to master. You may have the impression that law is a very cut and dried subject with black and white answers and no gray areas. You may be surprised to see that law is really not so cut and dried. Some legal questions have clear answers, some legal questions have unclear answers, and sometimes there is no answer at all. After all, if it was that simple, the world would not need lawyers.

One thing is certain: much of what you study will have no straightforward answer. The purpose of legal education is not to learn the rules that everyone agrees on, but to understand how to deal with situations where the rules are not agreed.

The law is not straightforward for a number of reasons. First, the law is there to govern people and people are not straightforward. The situations in which people find themselves are often complex, and a legal system that is strict and inflexible would lead to unjust decisions.

Second, tools of the law are words, and words have many different meanings.

Third, law does not operate in a vacuum to separate people from the ebb and flow of change in society. Law is a human tool, to be applied to human situations. As social, economic and environmental conditions change, so will the law (although not always at a desirable pace).

Finally, the law can be a tool of social change. Consider civil rights, employment law, advancement and protection of women and disadvantaged groups, incentives for small business, and environmental protection.

The primary aim of legal writing is to translate your legal thinking or reasoning into writing. You will spend a great deal of time and effort learning the process of legal reasoning—thinking about and analyzing the law—before you ever write or type a single word on the page or screen.

And the process of developing your legal reasoning skills will continue throughout your career.

Thinking in a legal analytical framework might make you the most annoying person at your Thanksgiving table, as you pontificate on the rules of a holiday meal and explain the reasons for the rules through illustration of prior family dinners, but your family will grow accustomed to your great analytical mind. Your family will forgive you down the road when they have a friend who is stopped for a traffic infraction or runs into trouble with a neighbor's bitey dog.

Let's get started.

PART I

Short & Happy
Legal History

Today's news is yesterday's history. Before we get down to the business of law school legal writing, it would do us well to take a look at groundwork for legal writing and place legal writing in the larger context of the U.S. laws. Legal analysis is the foundation of our country and all of the laws that create order and democracy. That is why excellent, clear, organized written communication is vital.

CHAPTER 1

Happy British Legal Roots: The British Documents That Shaped Our Legal System

We begin our journey across the Atlantic Ocean. As I am sure you are well-aware, our country's governing laws are rooted in English law. But you may not know that the primary source of American law is the following three British documents. If you studied these documents in history class, let's review:

A. Magna Carta, 1215: First Rights to the Populace

King James I[1] was the King of England from 1604 to 1625. Despite his commitment to peace and taking a pass on religious wars, he encountered serious conflicts with the British Parliament as a result of his "King-centered" values. James wrote these two missives, *The True Law of Free Monarchies*, and *Basilikon Doron* (*Royal Gift*), in which he argued that the God dictated that the King

---

[1]   King James VI of Scotland c. 1567, and then when Britain and Scotland united King James I of England.

was supreme ruler of the land. In the *True Law*, King James set for the theory of the divine right of kings, where he argued that kings are higher beings than other men for Biblical reasons. King James proposed an absolutist theory of monarchy, by which a king may impose new laws by royal prerogative but must also pay heed to tradition and to God, who would "stirre up such scourges as pleaseth him, for punishment of wicked kings."

Well, as you can probably imagine this king-centered theory did not sit well with the Barons in Parliament, the ruling class just under the king. So, the Barons got together and backed King James into a corner, and demanded things like "we're not paying you for our landholdings through military service." The Barons had the authority to kill the King and so-threatened. King James was faced with a serious dilemma: grant the barons certain rights or, well. . . die. King James chose life and thus was born the Magna Carta. The Magna Carta[2] [literal translation "big contract"] provided rights to the barons, including freedom of church, fair taxation, a right to a trial before imprisonment, due process, and the right to a common-law jury trial.

Fast forward 400-plus years [imagine the wavy lines] to the period of England known as The Enlightenment. Out of this period of, well, enlightenment regarding education and science, grew The Petition of Right.

King James died in 1625, and his son King Charles I, became King of England. King Charles named Sir Edward Coke, [pronounced "Cook," in case you are reading this book aloud as a bedtime story], High Sheriff of Buckinghamshire Following his father's example, Charles raised loans without Parliament's sanction and put citizens in debt prisons without trial. Coke told the Lords of Parliament that "Imprisonment in law is a civil death [and] a prison without a

---

[2]   Did you know: Rapper Jay Z named one of his albums after this very important document! (Magna Carta. . . Holy Grail 2013.)

prefixed time is a kind of hell." The Lords were non-plussed. Coke thus undertook the central role in framing and writing the Petition of Right.

The Petition of Right, approved in 1628, proclaimed various "rights and liberties" of free Englishmen, including a freedom from taxation without Parliamentary approval, the right of habeas corpus, a prohibition on soldiers being billeted in houses without the owner's will, and a prohibition on imposing martial law on civilians.

Parliament passed The Petition into formal law in 1641. The Petition became one of the three constitutional documents of English civil liberties, along with the Magna Carta and the Bill of Rights 1689 [to assemble and question government oversight], and quartering of troops [maintaining a national guard].

In the 17th Century, England also welcomed further reform in the way that the Crown regulated or oversaw the people.

The Toleration Act of 1689, although not applicable to certain religious groups, [Catholics for example] allowed the freedom to worship in England. The concepts expressed in this Act migrated to the United States with the English colonists, and formed the freedom of religion expressed in our Constitution.

B. Coming to America: The Colonies

Immigrants that formed the British Colonies in America brought with them the ideas contained in the documents that provided rights to British citizens and connected our British past to our current governing laws. The Colonists had certain freedoms to assert what was best for the colony. The following charters foretold our Constitution and Bill of Rights.

1. *Massachusetts Body of Liberties, 1641*

The Massachusetts Body of Liberties was the first legal code compiled by the English colonists when they arrived in New England. The Body of Liberties was one of the earliest documents to outline individual rights, such as a right to trial by jury, and a right against cruel and unusual punishment. Not surprisingly, the Bill of Rights later included many points from the Body of Liberties.

2. *Charter of Connecticut, 1662*

The Charter of Connecticut came about to rectify the fact that Connecticut lacked any legal governing doctrine in 1660 [Connecticut was officially founded in 1788]. Because Connecticut was a colony not recognized by the Crown [Charles II at the time], the governor of Connecticut sailed back to England [no easy journey, told to have taken over two months] with the Charter in hand pending the King's approval. The governor succeeded in his journey. Although the Charter concentrated more on property rights rather than individual rights, it was the first step in setting up a clear legal system for the settlers.

3. *Charter of Rhode Island and Providence Plantations, 1663*

The Rhode Island Charter outlined similar broad freedoms for its constituents but was far different in a major way: the Rhode Island Charter was the first charter to legally recognize the aboriginal people as being the true owners of the land.

Summary: American law and rights are rooted in British law and rights. Over time in Britain, the rights initially held only by the monarch reached first the [upper] class barons, and then during the period of The Enlightenment trickled down to regular folk. These rights traveled across the ocean to the Colonies and became the framework for our Constitution and Bill of Rights. And guess what? Our laws and rights are all recorded in writing.

CHAPTER 2

Happy State and Federal Courts

Because ultimately you will either be directly practicing in courts, accountable to the courts, or both, you should have a deep understanding of the history and organization of our judicial system. I will provide a brief background here, but you should do your own additional recon to fully understand your important role as an attorney in our court system.

One thing that causes confusion at the onset of law school is the dual court system, in other words, the federal and state court systems that govern our constituency. Each level of government has its own set of courts, at both the state and the federal level. As you will learn in your legal studies, some types of legal issues are resolved entirely in state courts, while other types of legal issue are handled entirely in federal courts. Not to confuse you more, but still other legal issues are handled in *both* state *and* federal courts.

Why is our court system so confusing?

A. Historical Context

Before the Constitution, the United States was governed by the Articles of Confederation [1781]. The Articles vested almost all functions of the national government in a single Congressional chamber. There was no separation of executive and legislative powers. [Uh-oh, I have a strange feeling of déjà vu].

As you were just thinking, the lack of separation between the executive and legislative branch became problematic. Remember what happened in England? When the kings had all the power over all of the laws? Kings made all the judgments? What happened to the constituency? Debt prisons. All sorts of other bad things. Correct.

Not having a national judiciary was considered a major weakness. Thus, in 1787, American delegates gathered at the Constitutional Convention in Philadelphia and began to discuss the development of a national judiciary. The Discussion was neither easy nor uniform: the first proposal, the Virginia Plan, set up both a federal Supreme Court and lower federal courts. Opponents devised the New Jersey Plan, which called for a single federal supreme court and no lower federal courts. New Jersey Plan delegates argued that state courts could hear all cases and that all appeals would go to the federal Supreme Court.

The conflict over the structure of the federal court system, vis-à-vis the state courts was resolved by compromise in the form of Article III of the Constitution: "The judicial Power of the United States, shall be vested in one supreme Court, and in such inferior Courts as the Congress may from time to time ordain and establish."

Article III Courts: Our federal circuit and district courts!

B. U.S. Supreme Court

The Judiciary Act of 1789 set up a judicial system with the Supreme Court as the final arbiter. The Supreme Court originally included a Chief Justice and five associate judges. The Supreme Court was created in conjunction with the unique federal form of government: although federal laws bound state courts, state courts could be the final arbiters of federal laws. The role of the Supreme Court was to interpret federal legislation.

C. Federal Circuit Courts of Appeals

The Judiciary Act of 1789 also created three circuit courts of appeals below the Supreme Court, each composed of two justices of the Supreme Court and a district judge. The circuit court would hold two sessions annually in each district within the circuit, and the two Supreme Court justices were expected to travel to the local areas and participate in the cases and were thus knows as "circuit riding judges."

The Justices hated their itinerant assignment. Thus, in 1793, Congress altered the circuit organization to include only one Supreme Court justice and one district judge. In 1801, Congress eliminated all circuit riding requirements and authorized the appointment of 16 new circuit judges, greatly extending the jurisdiction of the lower courts. But President Jefferson was pro-circuit riding, and in 1802, restored riding justice while at the same time expanding the number of circuits and providing that the circuit be presided over by a single district judge. Over time, the district judges assumed the responsibility for both district and circuit courts, the result being that both original and appellate jurisdiction were in the hands of district court judges.

Speaking of all these new circuit judges . . . .

D. *Marbury v. Madison* (1803)

You will study this case for weeks in your first semester of law school, and it will haunt you for the rest of your days, so I will provide merely a brief overview here.[1]

John Marshall was the Chief Justice of the Supreme Court from 1801–1835. Appointed to the Supreme Court by President Adams in the lame-duck days of his administration, Justice Marshall ran a tight ship and is responsible for the Supreme Court organization that we know of today. Marshall began the practice of handing down a single opinion rather than multiple separate [seriatim] opinions issued by separate judges. Marshall disliked dissention; in his opinion, a dissenting opinion undermined the Court's authority, so he urged justices to settle their differences privately and issue a single agreed upon opinion.

Marshall also was the first to use the court's power to make policy, declaring an act of Congress unconstitutional in *Marbury v. Madison*.

Marbury v. Madison involved a dispute over President Thomas Jefferson's refusal to deliver commissions of judges President John Adams appointed at the end of his term. [Hmmmm. Where have I heard of this problem before?] Adams named his Secretary of State, Marshall, to the Supreme Court, and the Senate confirmed the appointment. But time ran out and 17 commissions were not delivered before Jefferson's inauguration. William Marbury, one of the unconfirmed nominees asked the Supreme Court to force James Madison, Jefferson's Secretary of State, to deliver the commissions. Marbury relied on Section 13 of the Judiciary Act of 1789, which granted the Supreme Court the authority to issue *writs of mandamus*

---

[1] You can find a nice summary of the constitutional implications of *Marbury v. Madison* in A Short & Happy Guide to Constitutional Law.

[court orders] commanding a public official to perform an official, nondiscretionary duty.

But Marshall was faced with a predicament: should he disqualify himself because of his position under Adams? If the Supreme Court granted the *writ*, Jefferson would refuse to deliver the commissions and the Supreme Court would have no power to enforce the order. If Marshall refused to grant the *writ*, Jefferson would win.

To resolve the conundrum Marshall declared Section 13 of the Judiciary Act of 1789 unconstitutional, writing that Section 13 granted original jurisdiction to the Supreme Court in excess of that specified in Article III. *Marbury v. Madison* established what we know as **judicial review**: the Court's power to review and determine the constitutionality of Congressional acts.

E. Federal District Courts

Section 2 of the Judiciary Act of 1789 established 13 district courts as the trial courts of the federal judicial system. Each of the 11 states of the Union were deemed a district, and parts of Massachusetts and Virginia that later became Maine and Kentucky divided into separate districts [Hey! That's some interesting U.S. geography!]. As new states joined the Union, Congress created additional district courts. The organizational scheme established at that time still exists, following state boundary lines.

Over the centuries, with population growth [and growth in litigation] Congress periodically added districts and added judges to districts. As of May 2012, a total of 3,294 individuals had been appointed to federal judgeships, including 27 district court judges, 714 courts of appeals judges, 95 judges to the now-extinct 13 circuit courts, and 112 Supreme Court justices. There are currently 874 authorized Article III judgeships: nine on the Supreme Court, 179 on the courts of appeals, nine on the Court of International Trade and 677 for the district courts. Although the number of Supreme Court justices has remained the same for well over a century, the number of court of appeals judges has more than doubled since 1950, and the number of district court judges has increased more than three-fold in that time.

F. State Courts

State courts in each state generally mirror the hierarchy of the federal courts. At the trial level there are circuit or district courts. State appellate courts generally handle appeals[2] and the state supreme courts in the third tier hear a small number of secondary appeals.

Summary: After a lot of political infighting and disagreement, the leaders of our country ultimately settled on a parallel system of federal courts and state courts.

The Federal System is three-tiered, with the Supreme Court at the top as the final arbiter of federal claims, followed underneath by the Circuit Courts of Appeals. The original courts are the District courts that hold trials.

State court systems are similarly usually three-tiered, with a trial level, appellate level, and state supreme-court level.

To understand the types of written documents you will file and find in each of these courts, be sure to become familiar with the hierarchy of the court system and which court hears which kind of claim, as we will discuss in the next chapter.

---

[2] States have alternative names for their courts and some states have four tiers rather than three. Consult your jurisdiction of practice to learn about the form and function of the courts where you will be practicing law!

PART II

Sourcing and Citing the Law

Because legal analysis is grounded in authoritative support, we have to have a good handle on our sources of authority. We also need to be accountable to the original source of the authority and accurately communicate to our legal reader where on earth we found that earth shattering support for our thesis. These chapters introduce legal authority and legal citation.

CHAPTER 3

Happy Legal Authority: What Is Authority and How Is It Used?

A. Primary and Secondary Authority

There are two basic tiers of authority:

Primary authority is defined both as "case law" or "precedent opinions" of the court, (further explanation below) and as the written rules of law at the municipal, state, and federal level, such as statutes and ordinances (also explained below).

Secondary authority includes encyclopedic materials that explain or comment on areas of law such as law review articles, treatises, or hornbooks. Secondary authority is useful in helping you understand a particular legal topic or as a means of finding primary authority via aggregation.

B. Cases, Statutes, and Regulations: The Elevator Analogy

In terms of the first tier of authority, there are three types relevant to your written legal analyses: case law, statutes, and regulations.

Think of it this way: you are standing in the ground floor lobby of a three-story building. In order to write an effective and accurate legal analysis, imagine that you have to hop on the elevator and research all three floors of this building. (Disclaimer: depending on what you are writing and what your professor prefers, you may only need to hit one of the three floors.)

Legal authority is the term used to describe the sources of the law that you use to support a legal analysis.

More specifically:

1. First Floor: Precedent Cases

The U.S. legal system is a common law legal system (with a few State exceptions).[1]

What is a common law system, you ask? The common law began in England when there were no legislated laws (statutes). Instead of turning to statute books to assess the violation of a law or ordinance, the courts cumulated rules as they went along from the disposition of prior cases. Today much of our state law remains common law as opposed to statutory law. Examples of common law are plentiful and include battery, false imprisonment, trespass to land, negligence, defamation, and misrepresentation, just to name a few.

When a court follows the ruling of prior cases to issue a decision the court is using the principle of *stare decisis*, Latin for

---

[1]   Louisiana does not follow the common law.

"to stand by things decided," and better known as "precedent." Precedent reveals how the court decided legal issues in the past and provides guidance for how legal issues should be decided in current cases.

Your analysis of a particular legal issue or problem will be heavily dependent on precedent opinions or case law, comprising written opinions of the appellate review of a trial level case. Precedent is always at the heart of legal writing, whether for an inter-office memorandum assessing the viability or predicting the outcome of a client's case, or in a persuasive brief being written on behalf of your client for the courts.

You will hear precedent opinions referred to as "cases" throughout your law school and legal career, [Hey: you are reading *casebooks*!] but I refer to opinions of the court as precedent opinions to distinguish from active cases, meaning unresolved litigation before the various levels of court.

1L Pro-Tip

The most important skill to hone when reading several precedent opinions during your research is pinpointing what makes two or more precedents distinguishable or analogous from each other and applying those findings to your fact pattern.

---

2. *Second Floor: Statutes*

You have probably spotted a few statutes while reading precedent opinions on the first floor. If your legal issue is not a common law issue, it is likely a statutory issue.

Statutes are the laws drafted and enacted by the elected legislature at the state level and by Congress at the federal level. You probably saw the *School House Rock How a Bill Becomes a Law?* Well those are the basics, and you will discuss Statutes more in depth in your legal writing and research training. State and federal statutes are written and recorded in statute books and are also available in various online platforms. Municipal ordinances are the rules, regulations, or codes enacted into law by local government, as in cities and villages. Municipal ordinances include traffic regulations and housing regulations.

As noted above, Statutes are also considered to be primary authority, so spend time getting to know them—a good legal analysis depends on the court's interpretation of a statute.

3.   *Third Floor: Regulations*

Whereas Congress or state legislative branches draft statutes, Regulations are the rules and laws drafted and adopted by state and federal agencies. The Code of Federal Regulations (CFR) is the codification of the general and permanent rules and regulations (administrative law) published in the Federal Register by the executive departments and agencies of the federal government of the United States.

Regulations cover a wide range of laws from environmental protections to gambling laws. For example, the department of health and safety within a specific state will set out regulations regarding nursing home standards. Remember that many state agencies that provide regulations often overlap with their Federal counterpart.

C. Reading a Precedent Opinion aka "a Case"

One of the first, and most important skills you need to survive in law school and later as an attorney is the ability to quickly read and dissect a precedent opinion. There are 10 things you look for in a precedent opinion:

1. Title
2. Citation
3. Parties
4. Facts
5. Relevant Law
6. Legal Issues
7. Holdings
8. Reasoning
9. Separate Opinions
10. Ultimate Disposition (Judgment)

Before you begin to extract this information read your precedent opinion a minimum of **three times**. Each time you read through the opinion you will glean additional clarity to a new (and potentially confusing) set of facts and legal issues.

1. Title of Case

The title of the case will generally be *Name v. Name*, unless it is something along the lines of *In Re: Matter of Name*. The name of the person brought the lawsuit appears first.

2. Citation

The Citation is the location of the published opinion in the original book reporter, regional reporters, and additional publications. You will learn more about Citations, what they are, where they are, how to create citations, and how to use them in **Chapter 4.**

3. Parties

To fully understand the parties to the case, you will need to understand their legal positions.

In civil cases at the trial level (state circuit, district, or trial court/federal district court), the parties are known by their legal positions as **plaintiff** and **defendant** You will need to identify who sued who: **plaintiffs** sue **defendants.**

In criminal cases, the **government** (state or federal) becomes the **plaintiff,** and the accused is the **defendant.**

After the court makes a final determination, whether a civil judgment or a criminal conviction, the losing party may file an **appeal** for review in the second tier of the court system. The party positions changes to identify the filing party as the **appellant** and the opponent as the **appellee.**

But note: the parties retain the original position from their trial level dispute; even though the parties become appellant and appellee, it is best to continue to refer to the parties as plaintiff and defendant to avoid confusion over who sued who.

In administrative proceedings and in further proceedings at the Supreme Court level, the party seeking review of the trial court or appellate court determination is called the **petitioner** and the opponent is called the **respondent.**

4. *Facts and Procedural History*

Your case brief should include a summary of the background and legally relevant facts addressed by the court. You should include:

- A one-sentence description providing the background facts or story: What happened? Why are the parties in court?

- A summary of the procedural history in the lower courts, such as: the defendant convicted; the trial court granted summary judgment, etc.

5. Relevant Law

A statement of the relevant statute, ordinance, or common law principle that applies to the case, (the legally relevant facts) highlighting helpful key words or phrases.

6. Legal Issues

Provide a brief summary of the legal issues addressed by the court, for example, why the plaintiff brought the lawsuit and what common law or statute does the plaintiff argue that defendant violated or breached?

7. Holdings

The court's decision on the law is called the Holding. The Holding is specific to the facts of the case, in other words: "The defendant is liable to the plaintiff for injuries resulting from a dog bite." I will talk more about Holdings later.

8. Reasoning

The reasoning is the court's rationale or BECAUSE statement; the REASON for the court's Holding: "[HOLDING] The defendant is liable to the plaintiff for injuries resulting from a dog bite [REASONING] BECAUSE the defendant let Fido run out of the house in violation of the law prohibiting vicious animals from running loose in the streets."

9. Separate Opinions and Dicta

a. Concurring and Dissenting Opinions

Sometimes the judges or justices do not agree either on the Holding, the Reasoning, or both. These opinions are expressed as concurring (for example, judge agrees with the Holding but for a different reason) and dissenting opinions (disagrees with the Holding and Reasoning and believes the result should not stand. Note how each judge voted and the reasons for the judge's difference of opinion.

b.   Dicta

The other aspect of a court opinion you should watch for and make a note about is called *dicta*. Dicta is language the court writes that is not legally binding but provides a hypothetical that would call for a different holding were the facts to be different:

> "If Fido had been on a leash, the defendant would not be liable for injuries to the plaintiff. But those are not the facts of this case."

Dicta is not a holding but may be relevant to your client's case if your facts are different!

10. Ultimate Disposition

The ultimate disposition of the case is whether the lower court is "affirmed," or "reversed," or some combination of the two. Be careful not to confuse the ultimate disposition with the Holding, a common mistake made by law students and lawyers in practice!*

*Goal for Briefing Your Case Precedent: The FHR

FHR stands for Facts, Holding, and Reasoning. For each precedent case you brief, you want to reduce the information into one or two sentences that provide an executive summary of everything important to summarize the case. For example:

[FACTS] In a case where a poodle escaped out the front door of a defendant's home and bit a passerby on the ankle, the court [HOLDING] held that the defendant owner of the dog was liable to the injured plaintiff for damages [REASONING] because a pet owner is responsible for keeping a vicious pet on a leash in a public space.

CHAPTER 4

Happy Citations

I promised you that before we embarked on the components of a full legal analysis, we would take a little trip together. I call this trip:

A. Swimming with the Sharks[1]

Your writing professor just mentioned the word "citations." You just felt a wave of fear crash over you. You feel a bit like you were on the beach, enjoying your scenic vacation, when all of a sudden everyone is running back up to the beach yelling: "Sharks!" The fear is palatable. But here's the thing: citation sharks are actually your friends. After this chapter your sharks will become gentle dolphins,[2] and you will no longer harbor any fear about entering the water of citations.[3]

---

[1]   Thanks to Saloni Shah for assistance with this chapter concept.

[2]   Well, there are a few exceptions. http://www.theguardian.com/lifeand style/2014/oct/17/experience-i-was-attacked-by-a-dolphin.

[3]   This short lesson in citation is to allay your initial trepidation and acts merely as an introduction to the concept of citation. You will learn the intricacies of citation for all purposes of legal writing according to the rules of an additional guide, such as *The Bluebook: A Uniform System of Citation* or the *ALWD Guide to Legal Citation*.

We begin with an allegorical citation fairy tale:

Imagine winning an all-expense paid trip to Middelfart, Denmark, to go on a porpoise-watching excursion in the Lillbælt (Little Belt) that connects to the Baltic Sea.[4] You know no one in Middelfart, but you are a great swimmer and an even better explorer. You set off to Middelfart with a pair of neon, green, Nike shoes and an address for suite at a local Inn. After collectively spending twelve hours on a train, cab, and boat, you finally reach Middelfart. However, no one in Middelfart speaks English, and you fell behind with your Rosetta Stone Danish during your long travels.

You pull out your phone to "Google" your way to the Inn. But of course, in all that hustle, you forgot to change your data plan to an international plan. Now this is a nightmare. How are you going to get to the Inn? Lucky for you, you have a map and an address!

ADDRESS TO THE LAVISH MIDDELFART INN:

Skærbækvej 15, 2040
Middelfart, Denmark

*opfordre til hjælp
22260476490

"Wait," you exclaim, "I am the reader of this address and it makes no sense to me!"

Citations are like addresses in foreign languages. Providing a legal citation to a reader (*i.e.*, your professor, your supervisor, a judge's law clerk, a judge) is the same thing as providing a correct address to you, so that you can find your way to the Inn. Once you know the area or the language itself, you can easily navigate your way throughout the city. Likewise, citations are addresses for books

---

[4]   https://www.visitlillebaelt.com/ln-int/middelfart-fredericia/tourist.

and court opinions that you give to your readers so they can navigate their way to the legal opinion you cited.

There are five parts to an address: the name of the place, the number, the street name, the city and the state, and the zip code. We have an example of the address above. Let's now add an example of a citation:

> *Love v. Hate*, 17 S.W.3d 500 (Tex. Crim. App. 2000)

Step One: The Name

Where are we going? What are we looking for? What do we need to read? These are only some of the first questions that you should be thinking of when providing citations to published opinions. In the context of traveling, you would like to know the name of the place where you are going; likewise, it is important to know the name of the case. Unfortunately, if the case name is not as unique as Middelfart, but rather as generic as Love, you might find yourself with 1,000 cases to read rather than 10,000. Good job! We are getting closer to our citation destination.

Step Two: The Number

Traveling to another country is intimidating, especially when you do not speak the language and are not familiar with its infrastructure. Unlike how systematically some cities in the United States are created (using even numbered streets for North/South and odd numbers for East/West), that might not be true for Middelfart, Denmark. So in addition to having the name of the place you are heading to, it is important to have the street numbers. Similarly, citations require an address. If the street name, is generic, however, you might have narrowed the name down from 10,000 to 1,000 cases.

So what do the numbers mean? Do they have to be in a specific order? Does it matter? Well, the obvious answer is yes, it does matter, and otherwise you will never find the Inn.

In the foreign street address, the first part we have is: Skærbækvej 15. What does this mean? The word "Skærbækvej 15" is the name of the street: like Main Street. Congratulations! You have just figured out the first intersection.

In the citation example, the first number is: 17 S.W.3d. Now what does this mean? You may be doing your research on Westlaw, but the citations to legal opinions are actually tied to the publication of opinions in books. Perhaps you noticed tiny little numbers in the middle of sentences here and there within your Westlaw case? Those are the page numbers of the opinions as they appear in print in various volumes of different reporters! Several different vendors publish reporters of opinions. Usually one reporter is the official reporter, published by a particular state's official reporter of opinions. There are also regional reporters, which compile opinions from a set of states.

Imagine going into a library and all you have is the name of the book. Finding the book without a systematic format would not only be a daunting task, but almost impossible to find in an efficient manner. You will need to know the name of the publisher and in which volume the opinion is published.

In our example, "S.W.3d" stands for "South Western Reporter Third Series," and the "17" is the volume number of the third series of the South Western Reporter. The information we have so far means that the case you are looking for can be found ONLY in the jurisdiction of Arkansas, Kentucky, Missouri, Tennessee, or Texas. You have successfully cut down your search from 50 states to 5 states, and you know the opinion was published in the 17th volume of the third series of this reporter! You found this thick book in the library. You are almost there!

Step Two (A): The Number, Continued

But there is still more to the address. You have established only the first part of the intersection. There is more to find before you reach your final destination.

The other half of the address for Middelfart is: "2040." In this foreign address, you know that once you are at Skaerbaekvej15, you are going to keep walking on that road until you hit 2040, because that is your intersection. With this last step, you will find your Inn in a foreign country, and enjoy that free stay!

Can citations be just as easy? Yes! The rest of the number is: "500." This is the easiest part of the citation. This is the page number. Once you have selected the correct book, all you have left to do is tell the reader on what page the opinion may be located. You do not want the reader wasting time skimming through all the pages to find this particular opinion, especially after you already made the reader's life so much easier by telling her what book to select.

So far you have the volume, the reporter, and the page number. We found our citation address!

Step Three: The "Telephone" Number

Your citation let the reader know where to find the book, but because of the hierarchical system of courts, the reader is still not 100% sure that this opinion is relevant to his client's facts.

The remainder of the citation in the parenthesis, our "telephone number." tells the reader whether the opinion will be helpful in his court; in other words, provide "useful precedent." Here our telephone number is: (Tex. Crim. App. 2000).

The telephone number contains a lot of useful information. Like the area code, which reveals the sub-neighborhood you are calling within a particular state, the state abbreviation narrows down the state options. From the first abbreviation, the legal reader now knows that the opinion was issued in a Texas court.

The next abbreviation tells the reader what court this decision came from. Here, it is the criminal appellate court of Texas. The reader might be satisfied in knowing that the opinion generated from Texas and from the criminal appellate court. But there is one more important bit of information the reader needs to know: When was the opinion issued? Was it recent enough to be relevant? To answer this question, the last part of all citations includes the publication date.

You simplified the legal reader's life. Without looking up the opinion, the reader now knows if the opinion will be useful.

In summary, to give your legal reader the correct citation to a published opinion, you need to provide the following components:

1. Name
2. Volume of the Reporter
3. Reporter Name
4. Page Number
5. The Correct State and Court
6. The Date

The concept of citation is this simple. Through a correct citation, you are letting the reader know that you know the law and where to find it. You can now relax and enjoy and your porpoise-watching excursion!

1L Citation Pro-Tip: Tabbing

Once you learn the ropes of either the Bluebook[5] or the ALWD Guide,[6] you will want to tab your most used rules for ease of citation. Below are the **Most Frequently Used Rules** I recommend tabbing in the Bluebook and ALWD as follows:

Bluebook Blue & White Pages[7]

1. Signals
2. Order of Authority
3. Parenthetical
4. Subdivision
5. Short Form
6. Quotes
7. Omissions & Ellipses
8. Abbreviations, Numerals, & Symbols
9. Cases
10. Statutes
11. Constitutions
12. Legislative Materials
13. Books
14. Periodicals
15. Electronic
16. Unpublished Sources
17. Federal Court Tables
18. State Courts
19. Abbreviations—T6, T7

---

[5] The Bluebook: A Uniform System of Citation.

[6] Barger, *ALWD Guide to Legal Citation* (Wolters Kluwer, 6th Ed. 2017).

[7] I do not include the page numbers for the above cited Bluebook Rules because at the same time this book goes to press the Bluebook will release a new edition.

PART III

Happy Writing Structure

The beauty of writing and reading a legal analysis in an interoffice, predictive memorandum, is that we know how each document is organized. The framework for a legal analysis is recognized and memorized by every legal writer and reader and provides consistency in writing. Consistency also promotes efficiency. In these chapters we learn the basic structure of legal analysis for objective memos through a single legal writing assignment example.

CHAPTER 5

Components of Written Legal Communication

You now understand the background and foundation of our legal system, how the history intersects with legal practice, the types of legal authority, the way legal issues are expressed in writing, where to find authority, and how to tell your legal reader where you found your authority. You are thus ready to take on your own hypothetical client, begin to consider make your client's legal predicament, how you might resolve it, and communicate that result in writing.

This piece of writing you are to prepare is traditionally called the Legal Memo, Interoffice Memo, or Predictive Memo. In this assignment, you will analyze the legal problem, predict an outcome based on precedent, and make a recommendation for how the client should proceed, *i.e.*, provide legal advice.

When you receive your initial assignment of client facts, you will want to read the assignment or facts (sometimes also called the "prompt") as many times as you should read precedent case opinions, that is to say three times. As you read the prompt, you should take notes similar to the way you take notes on the precedent case for your brief:

1.   Who are the parties?

2.   Why are the parties in court?

3.   What happened? What are the facts?

4.   What is the applicable law?[1]

5.   How should the case be resolved?

I am going to provide a hypothetical assignment below. We will walk through the reading of the assignment to the preparation of the analysis section.

A.   Hypothetical Assignment (Prompt)

1.   Statute: *West Pacific Dog Bite Act*

In the State of West Pacific, a vicious pet owner is liable for any bite injuries incurred by a victim who is attacked in a public place. A vicious pet is any domesticated animal that has sharp teeth. A public place is defined as any area outside of the private property of the vicious pet owner. An owner is not liable for injuries to any party that taunts or provokes the owner's pet. 18 W.P.S § 107 (2012).

CLIENT FACTS: Mr. Pumpernickel owns a 3 lb. Chihuahua named Benedict. One day when Mr. Pumpernickel was puttering around the house and garden, Benedict escaped out of the front door and ran down the front sidewalk. Ms. Rye happened to be walking past Mr. Pumpernickel's house while texting on her mobile ePhone. Benedict ran up to Ms. Rye and attempted to snatch her

---

[1]   When you begin law school usually the applicable case precedent will be provided to you. After you become comfortable working with precedent you will learn to locate your own applicable precedent using legal research tools.

phone out of her hand with his mouth, like he does when Mr. Pumpernickel is not paying close attention. Startled, Ms. Rye recoiled, pulled her arm back, and Benedict's teeth chomped down on Ms. Rye's right wrist, rather than on her ePhone. Ms. Rye incurred a deep bite wound requiring five stitches.

ISSUE: Is Mr. Pumpernickel liable to Ms. Rye for her injuries as a result of Benedict's bite?

Now, how do we get started to organize our answer?

2. *Preview of Legal Memo*

You now know that your client is Ms. Rye and that she was attacked by a vicious chihuahua, Benedict, owned by Mr. Pumpernickel. You also know the law of the state of West Pacific. By looking at that simple fact pattern and statute you might think you know the answer.

But there is another piece: remember that **Authority Chapter** you just read? To articulate a successful legal analysis in writing you must explain:

1. The Thesis

2. The Facts (check),

3. Applicable Statute (check) and

4. Relevant Authority (Uh-oh: where is that?);

5. Extract a Rule or Synthesize a Rule from Multiple Precedent Cases (what does that mean?);

6. Explain the Rule from Precedent (HINT: the FHR)

7. Apply that Synthesized Rule to Your Client's Facts to

8. Predict a Legal Result and Provide Advice to the Mock Client.

Below are the two precedent opinions you will use to apply the law to your client's facts in order to predict a result. You will need to brief the cases. But look: I will show you how it's done below.

3.   *Precedent Case No. 1*

a.   *Sourdough v. Wheat,* **123 W.Pac 35 (2015)**

Justice Pecorino delivered the opinion of the court:

We are here today to decide whether an uninvited party guest is liable to the host of a party for injuries sustained as a result of the actions of the uninvited guest's canine companion.

The plaintiff, Sally Sourdough, hosted a garden party in for her friend Betty Bruchetta's 68th birthday in the common area Gazebo of the Bread Central Development. Although not invited, Sally's nosy neighbor, Wendy Wheat, decided to sneak in to the garden party to see if Sally's *hors d'oeuvres* were better than hers.

Wendy was accompanied by her dog, Cookie, a Fluffenpoof, specially bred for being a companionable presence and being calm in overwhelming situations. When Wendy entered Sally's party, the area around the Gazebo was rife with squirrels. Cookie became incensed at the presence of the squirrels, broke free from her leash, and darted toward an offending squirrel, but instead bore down on Sally's ankle. Sally sustained a torn ankle ligament as a result of the biting. Sally sued Wendy for money damages related to her injuries.

In the trial court, Sally argued that Wendy was liable for her injuries. Wendy argued that she was not liable because Cookie was not bred to inflict injuries.

Wendy's argument is inapposite, as the applicable statute does not contemplate the breeding aspects of an animal when determining liability.

In the state of West Pacific, "a vicious pet owner is liable for any bite injuries incurred by a victim who is attacked in a public place." 18 W.P.S § 107 (2012).

The statute defines a vicious pet is as "any domesticated animal that has sharp teeth." *Id.* The statute further defines a public place as "any area outside of the private property of the vicious pet owner." *Id.*

The trial court found Wendy Wheat liable to Sally Sourdough for damages inflicted by Cookie. We agree.

The biting incident detailed above occured on public property, *i.e.*, the common area Gazebo of Bread Central Development. The facts further reveal Cookie as a vicious animal under the statute, as she bit into the ankle of Sally Sourdough causing injuries that required hospital attention and five stitches.

Under the facts and circumstances, we hold Wheat liable for Cookie's actions, and affirm the judgment of the trial court.

Affirmed.

b.   Brief of Precedent Case No. 1

Now it's time for your to brief the precedent.

1.   **Title:** *Sourdough v. Wheat.*

2.   **Citation:** 123 W.Pac 35 (2015).

3.   **Parties:** Plaintiff: Sally Sourdough; Defendant: Wendy Wheat.

4.   **Facts:** Plaintiff Sally Sourdough, hosted a party in the common area Gazebo of the Bread Central Development. Wendy Wheat, an uninvited guest, sneaked into the party with her dog, Cookie, a Fluffenpoof, specially bred for being companionable and calm. Cookie broke free from her leash to chase a squirrel, but instead bit Sally's ankle. Sally sustained a torn ankle ligament.

5.   **Relevant Statute:** West Pacific Dog Bite Act, 18 W.P.S § 107 (2012), provides: "a vicious pet owner is liable for any bite injuries incurred by a victim who is attacked in a public place." The statute defines a vicious pet is as "any domesticated animal that has sharp teeth." The statute further defines a public place as "any area outside of the private property of the vicious pet owner."

6.   **Legal Issues:** Is Wendy liable to Sally under the W.P. Dog Bite Statute?

7.   **Holdings:** Yes, Wendy is liable to Sally.

8.   **Reasoning:** Wendy's dog Cookie is vicious because she had teeth sharp enough to bite Sally requiring stitches. The incident occurred in a public place.

9.   **Separate Opinions:** None.

10.   **Ultimate Disposition:** (Judgment): Affirmed trial court in favor of Sally.

4.   *Precedent Case No. 2*

a.   *Bagel v. Biali,* **456 W.Pac 45 (2018)**

Justice Parmesan delivered the opinion of the court:

We are here today to address a dispute regarding injuries incurred resulting from a dog bite. The following facts are relevant to our determination:

Bobby Bagel was out for drinks after work with his friends at Rounds, a City-owned outdoor brewpub. It was a warm day and he was wearing shorts.

Brenda Biali was also out at Rounds that day, and brought her golden retriever, Betsy, to meet a group of Ultimate Frisbee enthusiasts, and to plan their yearly conference. Rounds allows patrons to bring pets, as long as the pets are on a leash and do not intimidate children. Brenda gave Betsy's leash to another Ultimate enthusiast, Brian, while she went to grab drinks for the group. Brian was not paying attention and let go of the leash while miming a demonstration of his Ultimate throwing skills.

Bobby was sitting at the next table and does not like dogs. As Betsy nosed towards Bobby's table, Bobby splashed his beer on Betsy's nose, then reached around her and yanked at her tail. Betsy yelped and backed away, but when Bobby refused to let go of Betsy's tail she snarled, turned, and bit Bobby on his open kneecap, breaking the skin Brenda ran over to the scene immediately upon hearing Betsy snarling and Betsy retreated. Bobby required several stitches in his knee.

Bobby sued Brenda and Rounds for damages relating to his injuries. The trial court held neither Betsy nor Rounds were liable for damaged to Bobby under the West Pacific Dog Bite Statute. The court found that Rounds was a public space, and that Betsy was indeed a vicious animal. However, Brenda was not liable to Bobby because Bobby provoked Betsy.

We agree with the trial court.

Under the W.P. statute, "a vicious pet owner is liable for any bite injuries incurred by a victim who is attacked in a public place." 18 W.P.S § 107 (2012).

The statute defines a vicious pet is as "any domesticated animal that has sharp teeth." *Id.* The statute further defines a public place as "any area outside of the private property of the vicious pet owner." *Id.* In *Sourdough v. Wheat*, this court held the owner of a dog that bit a party host in a public place liable for injuries to that host. *Sourdough v. Wheat*, 123 W.P.2d 345.

There is no dispute here that Brenda's dog Betsy is vicious as defined under the statute and that the injuries were incurred in a public place.

However, the W.P. Statute further provides that "An owner is not liable for injuries to any party that taunts or teases the owner's pet." 18 W.P.S § 107 (2012). Thus, there is no liability to a plaintiff injured by a vicious dog in a public place when the injured party taunted or provoked the dog.

The trial court properly concluded that Bobby provoked Betsy by splashing her with beer and pulling on her tail. Brenda is not liable to Bobby for damages.

Affirmed.

b.   Brief of Precedent Case No. 2

    1.   **Title:** *Bagel v. Biali.*

    2.   **Citation:** 456 W.Pac 45 (2018).

    3.   **Parties:** Plaintiff: Bobby Bagel; Defendant: Brenda Biali.

    4.   **Facts:** Bobby Bagel was out for drinks at Rounds, a City owned outdoor brewpub. It was a warm day and he was wearing shorts. Brenda Biali was also out at Rounds with her golden retriever, Betsy. When Brenda was not looking, Betsy nosed towards Bobby's table. Bobby does not like dogs and he splashed his beer on Betsy's nose, then reached around her and yanked at her tail. Betsy yelped and backed away, but when Bobby refused to let go of Betsy's tail she snarled, turned, and bit Bobby on his open kneecap, breaking the skin Brenda ran over to the scene immediately upon hearing Betsy snarling and Betsy retreated. Bobby required several stitches in his knee.

    5.   **Relevant Law:** The West Pacific Dog Bite Act provides "a vicious pet owner is liable for any bite injuries incurred by a victim who is attacked in a public place." 18 W.P.S § 107 (2012). The statute defines a vicious pet is as "any domesticated animal that has sharp teeth." Id. The statute further defines a public place as "any area outside of the private property of the vicious pet owner."

Id. W.P. Statute further provides that "An owner is not liable for injuries to any party that taunts or teases the owner's pet." 18 W.P.S § 107 (2012).

Precedent interprets the statutory authority: In *Sourdough v. Wheat*, this court held the owner of a dog that bit a party host in a public place liable for injuries to that host. *Sourdough v. Wheat*, 123 W.P.2d 345.

6.   **Legal Issues:** Is Brenda liable to Bobby under the W.P. Dog Bite Statute?

7.   **Holdings:** Brenda is not liable to Bobby for bite injuries by Betsy.

8.   **Reasoning:** Although Betsy is defined as vicious and Rounds is a public place under the statute, Bobby provoked Betsy.

9.   **Separate Opinions:** None.

10.   **Ultimate Disposition (Judgment):** Affirms judgment of trial court.

Now that you have all of the information you need to support your legal analysis, how in the Sam Hill do you put it all together? In other words: How do you apply the law to your client's facts to make a prediction and provide a recommendation?

We need to construct one more summary, let's call it a compilation of both your client's facts and the law and rules from your precedent cases. You will use these notes in the next phase:

B. Compilation of Facts and Rules

1.   **Thesis:** Mr. Pumpernickel is liable to Ms. Rye for dog bite injuries.

2.   Client **Facts:** Mr. Pumpernickel owns a 3 lb. Chihuahua named Benedict. One day when Mr. Pumpernickel was puttering around the house and garden, Benedict escaped out of the front door and ran down the front sidewalk. Ms. Rye happened to be walking past Mr. Pumpernickel's house while texting on her mobile ePhone. Benedict ran up to Ms. Rye and attempted to snatch her phone out of her hand with his mouth, like he does when Mr. Pumpernickel is not paying close attention. Startled, Ms. Rye recoiled, pulled her arm back, and Benedict's teeth chomped down on Ms. Rye's right wrist, rather than on her ePhone. Ms. Rye incurred a deep bite wound requiring five stitches.

3.   Applicable **Statute:** West Pacific Dog Bite Act, 18 W.P.S § 107 (2012).

The owner of a vicious pet is liable for any bite injuries incurred by a victim who is attacked in a public place. A vicious pet is any domesticated animal that has sharp teeth. A public place is defined as any area outside of the private property of the vicious pet owner. An owner is not liable for injuries to any party who taunts or provokes the owner's pet. 18 W.P.S § 107 (2012).

4.   **Relevant Authority:** *Sourdough v. Wheat*, 123 W.Pac 35 (2015); *Bagel v. Biali*, 456 W.Pac 45 (2018).

5.   **Find a Controlling Rule** and **Synthesize a Rule** from multiple precedent opinion: What do I mean by *extract* and *synthesize?* I will spend some time here on Number 4 to explain these important concepts.

A.   Find the Controlling Rule

Finding or extracting the relevant rule or rules that we use to formulate a legal analysis can be a bit overwhelming and complicated. That is because there are several different types of rules in the mix.

First we need to find the **Controlling Rule**, which can be either a **statute** or the **common law**. The controlling rule provides the backdrop of the legal issue and is generally either prescriptive or proscriptive: **Proscriptive rules prohibit** certain acts or behavior and tell you what cannot do. Proscriptive rules will provide penalties or punishments for breaking those rules. Sometimes proscriptons are in the form of bans:

> "Food service businesses are prohibited from using plastic straws and plastic utensils in Seattle."[2]

By contrast, **prescriptive rules delineate conduct**, what you are required to do or how you are required to behave in certain circumstances. For example:

> "All residents living in single-family structures, multifamily structures, and mixed-use buildings shall separate paper, cardboard, glass and plastic bottles and jars, aluminum and tin cans, food waste, and compostable paper for recycling, and no paper, cardboard, glass or plastic bottles and jars, aluminum or tin cans, food waste, or compostable paper shall be deposited in a garbage container or drop box or disposed as garbage at the City's transfer stations."[3]

When a **statute** controls your client's issue, the statute is the controlling rule. However, the statute is not the Rule that you will

---

[2]   Seattle's Food Serviceware Requirements, SMC 21.36.086.
[3]   Residential recycling required 21.36.083.

use to analyze your client's legal issue; we look to the judicial interpretation of the controlling statute in the form of precedent.

Similarly, your client's issue may be controlled by a **common law rule**. A common law rule is not a statute, but similarly controls the legal issue. Colorado's common law regarding adverse possession provides as follows:

> "To obtain title by adverse possession, a party must establish by a preponderance of the evidence that his possession was actual, adverse, hostile, under a claim of right, exclusive, and uninterrupted for the statutory period."[4]

You probably noticed that the common law rule above is subject to a *statute* of limitations, so there is a statutory component to the common law rule. But proof of adverse possession is a common law inquiry.

B. Examine Components of Controlling Rule

Once you know whether your client's legal issue is governed either by statute or by common law, you need to look at the requirements of the controlling rule: does the rule require fulfillment of certain or all *elements* to prove a violation of a criminal offense or to assign liability?

1. Elements

Elements are all of the conditions that *must* be fulfilled to establish that the controlling rule is fulfilled.

For example, the statute in our dog bite case requires that *all* of the following elements be proved for liability to inure:

---

[4]   *Welsch v. Smith*, 113 P.3d 1284, 1287 (Colo. App. 2005).

1. A vicious pet with sharp teeth;

2. a bite injury; *and*

3. injury incurred in a public place

To prove an owner's liability for an animal bite under the controlling statute, a plaintiff *must* prove all three of the elements listed above: the pet is vicious, the plaintiff incurred a bite injury, the plaintiff was in a public space at the time.

To determine whether all of the elements are required to prove liability or a criminal offense, look to the *operative words.* Operative language is usually in the form of **and** or **or.** If a statute delineates elements connected by the word **and**, all of the elements must be established to make a claim or prove an offense. If the statute separates some of the elements by **or** not all of the elements must be proved to make a claim.

Operative words can also act as exceptions even if all of the elements are proved. For example, the last sentence of the dog bite statute provides: "an owner is not liable for injuries to any party who taunts or provokes the owner's pet." The last sentence is an *exception* to the controlling rule: the pet owner is not liable for injuries incurred **if** the plaintiff taunted the pet.

2. *Factors*

By contrast, a statute or common law controlling rule may not have required elements that must all be met, but rather a series of *factors* the court will take into account to prove violation or liability of a controlling rule.

For example, an independent contractor is "any person who does work for another, under conditions which are not sufficient to make him a servant of the other."[5] Courts consider numerous

---

[5] (Second) of Agency § 220(2) (1958).

*factors de*fining a "servant" to determine whether a worker is an independent contractor:

(a)   the extent of control which, by the agreement, the master may exercise over the details of the work;

(b)   whether or not the one employed is engaged in a distinct occupation or business;

(c)   the kind of occupation, with reference to whether, in the locality, the work is usually done under the direction of the employer or by a specialist without supervision;

(d)   the skill required in the particular occupation;

(e)   whether the employer or the workman supplies the instrumentalities, tools, and the place of work for the person doing the work;

(f)   the length of time for which the person is employed;

(g)   the method of payment, whether by the time or by the job;

(h)   whether or not the work is a part of the regular business of the employer;

(i)   whether or not the parties believe they are creating the relation of master and servant; and

(j)   whether the principal is or is not in business.[6]

Other than the first factor, the extent of control, which traditionally courts weigh heavily in each legal analysis regarding an independent contractor a party to a lawsuit need not prove all of the remaining nine factors. Courts will examine the evidence provided by both parties and weigh the strength of the factors presented by each

---

[6]   *Powell v. Tanner*, 59 P.3d 246, 249 (Alaska 2002).

party against the other to decide whether the condition of independent contractor status exists.

C.   Synthesize a Rule from Multiple Precedents

You read two precedent opinions (cases) reported out of the West Pacific Court. Do you see anything in common between the precedent in my case briefs? Look to where I summarized the law.

In the first case, *Sourdough*, the court interprets the statute and holds that the defendant is liable for damages to the injured party. But in the second case, *Bagel*, the court finds that the defendant is not liable.

Why is the defendant not liable?

In reaching the conclusion against liability, the *Bagel* court cites the *Sourdough* precedent, specifically acknowledging that the *Sourdough* court found the defendant liable in a similar situation. But were the scenarios identical? Turns out, no, because in *Bagel* the injured plaintiff taunted and provoked the dog (like you did to your little sister or brother, admit it) and the statute specifically provides that liability will not inure against a defendant where the plaintiff provoked the dog.

When we *synthesize* a rule, we are looking to provide summary of the *court's interpretation of the controlling statute or common law* from one or multiple precedent opinions. We are not seeking to restate or quote the statute again. Why not provide the statute as the rule? Remember when we talked about the meaning of precedent? Our system of precedent or case law depends on the court's interpretation of the statute, in other words, we show not just what the statute requires, but how the statute was *applied* in prior (precedent) legal situations.

Our **Synthesized Rule** in this instance is extracted from the two precedent cases you read above and may look something like this:

RULE: A dog owner is liable for injuries to another person when the dog bites that person and both the dog and the injured party are on public property. *Sourdough v. Wheat*, 123 W.Pac 35 (2015). However, even if the dog bites a person and both parties and the dog are on public property, a dog owner is not liable for injuries when that injured person provokes and taunts the dog thereby causing the biting behavior. *Bagel v. Biali*, 456 W.Pac 45 (2018).

6.   Explain the Rule

Right above when we provided our Synthesized Rule, we cited the two precedent cases in support. Our legal reader may be wondering: "Hmmm. I wonder what happened in that *Sourdough* case and in that *Bagel* case? I wonder if we need to know what happened in those cases in order to figure out what should happen in our client's case?"

The answer to that last question is: **Yes.**

The method here is the **FHR.** Remember the **FHR?** Facts, Holding, and Reasoning? The FHR provides your **Explanation** of the **Synthesized Rule**, in other words, the facts and law that *explain* the ultimate rule.

Let's have a crack at the **Explanation**, and mark the components for clarity:

FACTS: Where a homeowner hosted a party in a common area of a homeowner development, and an uninvited guest brought a dog that bit the homeowner causing injuries, **HOLDING:** the uninvited guest is liable for to the homeowner for damages **REASONING:** because the dog was vicious and the injuries occurred in a public place. *Sourdough v. Wheat*, 123 W.P.2d 345.

By contrast, **FACTS:** A pet-owner in a public setting, whose dog bites a patron, **HOLDING:** is not liable for injuries to the patron **REASONING:** when that patron taunted and provoked the dog into biting. *Bagel v. Biali*, 456 W.Pac 45 (2018).

Returning to the outline of our legal analysis:

7. Apply That Synthesized Rule to Your Client's Facts

The Application of the Synthesized Rule to your Client's facts has its own sub-framework as follows:

1. Conclude on the Synthesized Rule

2. Compare or contrast (or both) the precedent case factsto your client's facts

3. Provide additional supporting fact (if any)

4. Provide counter-application of Synthesized Rule

5. Re-Conclude.

Let's see how this Application looks:

Conclusion on the Synthesized Rule: The court will likely find Mr. Pumpernickel liable to Ms. Rye for bites by his vicious dog, Benedict, because Ms. Rye was on public property at the time and did not taunt Benedict.

Compare to Precedent: Like in *Sourdough*, where the dog bit the homeowner at a party in a public garden, Benedict bit Ms. Rye when she was on the public sidewalk. Unlike *Bagel*, however, where the bar patron taunted the dog resulting in a bite injury, here Ms. Rye did not taunt Benedict prior to being bitten.

Expand on Supporting Facts: Here, Ms. Rye was merely walking on the public crosswalk when Benedict dashed out from Mr. Pumpernickel's house. Ms. Rye did nothing to aggravate or provoke Benedict.

Counter Application: The court could find that in holding her ePhone, Ms. Rye provoked Benedict because Benedict was drawn to the reflection of the light off of the phone screen, but this conclusion is unlikely, as merely holding a phone is not provocation under the statute or the precedent. In *Bagel*, the bar patron intentionally spilled beer on the dog's nose and also intentionally pulled the dog's tail. *Bagel*, 456 W.Pac at 45.

Conclusion: Mr. Pumpernickel is liable for Ms. Rye's damages.

8. Predict a Legal Result and Provide Advice to the Mock Client

Here you provide a short conclusion and potentially some advice to the client based on your entire analysis:

> "Mr. Pumpernickel allowed Benedict to run unrestrained on public property providing the opportunity for Benedict to bite Ms. Rye. Ms. Rye did nothing to provoke Benedict. The court will therefore likely find Mr. Pumpernickel liable for damages to Ms. Rye for her injuries, and the client should proceed with the claim."

In the next few chapters we will assemble all of these parts to see what a Legal Memo really looks like.

CHAPTER 6

Small Scale Container: The Discussion/ Analysis Section of the Legal Memo

To prepare a successful written legal analysis, you will need to use a solid organizational structure. Your legal analysis needs to be communicated in a framework that the legal reader will understand and in the order that the reader expects to encounter the information. Throughout the remainder of your legal life, you will happily write the Discussion or Analysis section of your memos and briefs in some form of one of these legal frameworks. (There are other sections necessary to a complete a Legal Memo; those are discussed below in the Large Scale Container Chapter.)

The framework for organizing the Analysis or Discussion portion of a written memo is often referred to as "Small Scale Organization." The following chart provides some of the more commonly used frameworks for this Small Scale Organization of the Discussion or Analysis section in a Legal Memo:

Issue	Conclusion	Conclusion	Thesis	Issue
Rule	Rule	Rule	Rule	Rule
Application	Explanation	Application	Explanation	Analysis
Conclusion[1]	Application	Conclusion[2]	Analysis	Rebuttal
	Conclusion		Conclusion	Conclusion
			Counter-Application	

Providing your legal analysis in one of these frameworks maximizes reader comprehension and reflects your legal reasoning.

I teach the TREACC framework, and I will provide an example below using TREACC to analyze our client's case *vis-a-vis* the applicable precedent. You will notice that I insert the initial letter from each component of the framework in parentheses prior to each example of that component. I advise that when you are first getting started drafting your analyses that you mark your TREACCs in the manner I describe. Marking each component will insure that you included the proper information in each section and will also alert your legal reader that you are writing within the framework.

A. Inside the Application Studio: TREACC Explained

Now we are going to use all of our our organized notes from Chapter 4 and insert them into the TREACC framework. It should look pretty similar to what we constructed in the last chapter, but with the components specified:

---

[1] In my opinion, the IRAC format should be reserved for exam-writing, but some writing programs and or professors teach the IRAC paradigm to organize a legal analysis.

[2] Framework for persuasive legal briefs.

1. Thesis

The thesis is your prediction of the court's outcome on the element of a statute or law or legal issue. The thesis is not cited to authority because it is your personal conclusion. The thesis will look something like this:

(T) The court will likely find Mr. Pumpernickel liable for injuries to Ms. Rye as a result of Benedict's bite.

2. Rule

The Rule is the announcement of the rule that court will use to resolve the legal issue. You will cite the rule to the precedent authority. *If there is a statute, the statute is not the Rule.* The statute is the guiding principal or underlying *governing* rule, but is not the Rule. Remember that in the U.S. legal system the Rule the court applies is derived from *precedent*; the Rule is synthesized from precedent that interprets the rule, as we practiced in Chapter 4.

The Rule will look like the Synthesized Rule we put together:

(R) A dog owner is liable for injuries to another person when the dog bites that person and both the dog and the injured party are on public property. *Sourdough v. Wheat*, 123 W.P.2d 345 (2015) However, even if the dog bites a person and both parties and the dog are on public property, a dog owner is not liable for injuries when that injured person provokes and taunts the dog thereby causing the biting behavior. *Bagel v. Biali*, 456 W.Pac 45 (2018).

The Thesis plus the Rule will look something like this:

(T) The court will likely find Mr. Pumpernickel liable for injuries to Ms. Rye as a result of Benedict's bite. (R) A dog owner is liable for injuries to another person when the dog bites that person and both the dog and the injured party are on public property.

Sourdough v. Wheat. However, even if the dog bites a person and both parties and the dog are on public property, a dog owner is not liable for injuries when that injured person provokes and taunts the dog thereby causing the biting behavior. *Bagel v. Biali,* 456 W.Pac 45 (2018).

3. Explanation

The Explanation illustrates the precedent case or cases from which you extracted the rule or the **FHR:** the Facts of the precedent case plus the legal Holding, and the Reason for the Holding. The Explanation is usually one or two sentences and is always cited.

Here are two examples of an Explanation:

(E)   In *Sourdough,* [FACTS] where the dog was on private property [REASONING] when it bit Mr. Sourdough, the court [HOLDING] held that the owner Ms. Wheat was not liable for Mr. Sourdough's injuries. *Sourdough v. Wheat,* 123 W.Pac 35, 36 (2018).

You might also find the *In-held-when* format helpful to articulate the Explanation:

(E)   [FACTS] **In** a case **where** a vicious teeth baring pet bit a victim [HOLDING] the pet owner was not liable for injuries under the W. Pac statute [REASONING] **when** the victim provoked the animal. *Bagel v. Biali,* 456 W.Pac 45, 47 (2015).

Most of the time, that one sentence is all you need. However, you should **provide more explanation** with factually complicated precedent, significant precedent, and descriptions of the evolution of the law if there are many precedent cases addressing the issue over a long period of time.

4. Application

The Application is the Prediction on the Rule, compared to and/or contrasted from the Precedent case Explanation. There is generally no citataion to authority in the Application because this is your own analysis; your application of rule and precedent case to your client's facts cannot be found within the precedent cases.

Begin the Application with a **prediction or conclusion on the Rule**, not on the entire claim for example:

(A)   Benedict was on public property when he bit Ms. Rye's arm.

The mini-thesis above reflects both the conclusion on viciousness and on the issue of public/private property.

Then compare and contrast your client's case to the precedent cases using the explanations you articulated above to apply the precedent (we did this in Chapter 4, too!):

(A)   Unlike *Soughdough*, where the dog was on private property when it bit the victim, here Benedict was on the public sidewalk when it bit Ms. Rye. Also, in contrast to *Bagel*, where the dog bite the Mr. Biali because Mr. Biali taunted the dog, Ms. Rye did not taunt Benedict.

5.   *Counter-Application*

The Counter-Application is an alternative prediction of the rule as applied to the client's facts based on the same articulated rules and precedent cases: in other words, the court could apply the same rule and reach the opposite conclusion. (Depending on clarity or the ambiguity of your authority, a counter-application may not be necessary. You will need to read the precedent very carefully.) You provide a thesis that is the opposite conclusion of your original Thesis, followed by a Rebuttal that supports your original Thesis, and then a brief conclusion.

A Counter-Application would look like this:

(C/A)   [COUNTER-THESIS/CONCLUSION] The court might find that Mr. Pumpernickel is not liable to Ms. Rye for injuries to her hand because she aggravated Benedict by flashing her ePhone at him. [SUPPORT FROM PRECEDENT] In *Bagel* the court held that Mr. Bagel taunted the dog, Betsy, before she lunged at him. [REBUTTAL] However, it is not likely that the court would find that holding a cellphone and having the light catch the screen is taunting a vicious pet. [RETURN TO YOUR ORIGINAL CONCLUSION] The court would therefore find Mr. Pumpernickel liable.

6.   *Conclusion*

Finally, you will want to conclude your legal analysis by re-stating your Thesis, along with providing information on potential legal consequences.

A Conclusion might look like this:

(C)   The court will find that Mr. Pumpernickel is responsible to Ms. Rye for injuries incurred as a result of being bitten by Benedict, and is liable for money damages. The client should move ahead with the case against Mr. Pumpernickel.

Now that we have an idea about how to construct the Discussion section, we will see how the Discussion fits into the whole memo.

CHAPTER 7

Happy Large Scale Organization: The Memo Container

In Chapters 4 and 5 we spent time compiling the information necessary to construct our legal analysis for the Interoffice or Predictive Memo. We organized the Discussion/Analysis section according to the TREACC framework, which I called the Small Scale Organization. But we are not yet finished, because we do not have a complete memo. Where do you put the other information, like the client facts? How do we let the legal reader know what this memo is all about?

We need another Container to make the Memo whole: the Large Scale Organization.

Below, I will discuss two Containers for your analysis of Ms. Rye's potential dog bite claim. First, the Interoffice or Predictive Memo. Second, a shorter method of communication: the email memo or e-memo.

A. Interoffice/Predictive Memos

Predictive or Interoffice Office Memos, the legal communication you have been working on up to this point, usually contain the following components or sections:

I.   CAPTION

II.   INTRODUCTION/OVERVIEW or QUESTION & BRIEF ANSWER

III. FACTS

IV. RELEVANT STATUTE (IF ANY)

V.   DISCUSSION

     > **TREACC GOES HERE** <

VI. CONCLUSION ("BIG C")

Now we will take the case of Ms. Rye versus Mr. Pumpernickel and put together everything we worked on together in Chapters 4 and 5 and see what the full office memo will look like. Below is an annotated memo (notes in the margins) explaining the components we learned above.

MEMORANDUM

TO: Litigation Partner

From: First Year Associate

RE: Dog Bite Claim/Ms. Rye

Date: Today's Date, Any Year

OVERVIEW

Our client, Ms. Rye, would like to know the viability of a potential personal injury claim against Mr. Pumpernickel for damages associated with dog bite injuries Ms. Rye sustained. Based on the West Pacific Dog Bite Act and relevant precedent, the client will likely succeed in a case for damages against Mr. Pumpernickel.

FACTS

Mr. Pumpernickel owns a three-pound Chihuahua named Benedict. One day when Mr. Pumpernickel was puttering around the house and garden, Benedict escaped out of the front door and ran down the front sidewalk. Ms. Rye happened to be walking past Mr. Pumpernickel's house while texting on her mobile ePhone. Benedict ran up to Ms. Rye and attempted to snatch her phone out of her hand with his mouth, like he does when Mr. Pumpernickel is not paying close attention. Startled, Ms. Rye recoiled, pulled her arm back, and Benedict's teeth chomped down on Ms. Rye's right wrist, rather than on her ePhone. Ms. Rye incurred a deep bite wound requiring five stitches.

APPLICABLE STATUTE

In the State of West Pacific, a vicious pet owner is liable for any bite injuries incurred by a victim who is attacked in a public place. A vicious pet is any domesticated animal that has sharp teeth. A public place is defined as any area outside of the private property of the vicious pet owner. An owner is not liable for injuries to any party that taunts or provokes the owner's pet. 18 W.P.S § 107 (2012).

DISCUSSION

(T) The court will likely find Mr. Pumperickel liable for injuries to Ms. Rye as a reult of Benedict's bite.

(R) A dog owner is liable for injuries to another person when the dog bites that person and both the dog and the injured party are on public property. *Sourdough v. Wheat*, 123 W.Pac 35 (2015). However, even if the dog bites a person and both parties and the dog are on public property, a dog owner is not liable for injuries when that injured person provokes and taunts the dog thereby causing the biting behavior. *Bagel v. Biali*, 456 W.Pac 45 (2018).

(E) For example, where a homeowner hosted a party in a common area of a homeowner development, and an univited guest brought a dog that bit the homeowner causing injuries, the uninvited guest is liable for to the homeowner for damages because the dog was vicious and the injuries occured in a public place. *Sourdough v. Wheat*, 123 W.Pac 35.

By contrast, a pet-owner in a public setting whose dog bit a patron was not liable for injuries to the patron when that patron taunted and provoked the dog into biting. *Bagel v. Biali*, 456 W.Pac 45.

(A) Benedict was on public property when he bit Ms. Rye's arm. Unlike *Soughdough*, where the dog was on private property when it bit the victim, here Benedict was on the public sidewalk when it bit Ms. Rye. Also, in contrast to *Bagel*, where the dog bite the Mr. Biali becaues Mr. Biali taunted the dog, Ms. Rye did not taunt Benedict.

(C/A) The court might find that Mr. Pumpernickel is not liable to Ms. Rye for injuries to her hand because she aggravated Benedict by flashing her ePhone at him. In *Bagel* the court held that Mr. Bagel taunted the dog, Betsy, before she lunged at him. However, it is not likely that the court would find that holding a cellphone and having the light catch the screen is taunting a vicious pet. The court would therefore find Mr. Pumpernickel liable.

CONCLUSION

The court will find that Mr. Pumpernickel is responsible to Ms. Rye for injuries incured as a result of being bitten by Benedict and is liable To Ms. Rye for money damages. The client should move ahead with the case against Mr. Pumpernickel.

B. E-Memos

Another way you might communicate the same analysis to your client in an expedited manner is via the shorter "E-memo" format.

The E-memo includes the following components:

- Subject line that reveals legal conclusion
- Identify the parties and their relationship to each other
- Brief summary of the facts and the reason you are providing the analysis ("You asked me . . .")
- Identify Applicable statute (If any)
- Apply applicable precedent authority
- Provide ideas for next steps/offer to provide additional information

Let's see how an E-memo for Ms. Rye's potential case might look:

Today 4:47 PM

Deborah Borman

Ms. Rye Has Valid Claim for Dog Bite

Partner:

You asked me to assess the viability of our client Ms. Rye's potential claim against Mr. Pumpernickel for injuries associated with a dog bite.

After reviewing the applicable statute and precedent case law, I conclude that Ms. Rye has a valid claim.

Under W.P. law, a pet owner is liable for for any bite injuries to a victim attacked in a public place. A pet owner is not liable for the injuries, however, if the victim taunted or provoked the pet. 18 W.P.S. § 107 (2012).

Mr. Pumpernickel's dog Benedict bit Ms. Rye when she was on the public sidewalk in front of Mr. Pumpernickel's house. Ms. Rye was texting on her cellphone at the time of the incident and did not see the dog approach her. Ms. Rye's deep wound necessitated five stitches to her hand.

In prior W. Pac cases, a dog owner was liable to a victim when the dog bit the victim at a party on public property (*Sourdough v. Wheat*), but not when the bite was a result of the victim taunting and provoking the dog. *Bagel v. Biali*.

Here, Ms Rye was on public property, she was seriously injured by the bite and she did not provoke Mr. Pumpernickel's dog. A court would not likely find that carrying a cell phone provokes a dog to bite.

Ms. Rye has a good claim for damages and we should proceed to file the complaint.

Please let me know if you would like any additional information on this matter.

Warmly,

Deborah Borman

--
Associate
Law Firm
Anytown, West Pacific

C. Texts with Client

In today's world of virtual, immediate communication, attorneys are increasingly faced with the challenge of engaging with clients via text message. As I am sure you are well aware, texting is now one of the most common forms of communication. Your client will likely first engage you via an initial consultation in person. You may then have follow up conversations via email, phone, and maybe video conferencing.

After you agree to work with a client, however, you may find that your client will send text messages for convenience and to obtain an immediate response. Sometimes client text messages are short questions about scheduling or timing like "what courtroom is the hearing in today?"

At other times, however, because of a feeling of urgency about their legal matter, clients may text pertinent details, evidence, or even photos related to their legal claim.

When you and your client exchange text messages, you must consider both confidentiality and record keeping. How do you keep a substantive text message confidential? What is the best method to save and print all client-related text message conversations?

Because there is still no foolproof method of saving text messages, I suggest nipping substantive legal exchanges via text messaging in the proverbial bud:

●●●○○ Sprint LTE   11:05 PM   75% ⬛️⫸

❮ Messages   **Louise E.**   Details

> Are you available to change our Tuesday afternoon meeting to Monday?

> Let me check my calendar; what time did you have in mind?

> 2:00 would be best.

> In the meantime, HR wants to talk to me on Friday about my harassment claim. Do you think I should share the details about my prior relationship with my supervisor during that meeting?

> Please call me at your earliest convenience. It is best for your case to discuss your issues confidentially over the phone or in person at our meeting. Also, I suggest that you delete this message thread. I have our appointment memorialized in my calendar.

> **Pro-Tip**
>
> You now have all the tools necessary to create and organize a legal analysis for an Interoffice or Predictive Memo, an E-memo or respond to a client text message.

Note that the sample and tips provided in Chapters 4 and 5 do not include methods of doing your own legal research. The organization and framework are provided in a "closed universe" manner, similar to the way precedent and statutes will be provided to you to complete your initial written analysis assignments. I will provide some preliminary research tips for you in Chapter 11.

PART IV

Happy Persuasive Briefs

This section is devoted to the construction and content of persuasive briefs. Here, I illustrate the differences between a predictive memo and a persuasive brief using real examples from Seventh Circuit filings in a single case and provide an alternative framework for your persuasive court filing.

May You Please the Court

Now that you are an expert on constructing a predictive legal analysis and know how to organize your Interoffice written communication into a framework that is easily recognizable to every legal reader, you are ready to dig into the structure of court filings or briefs.

A. Legal Briefs Filed in Court

Legal briefs are quite similar to your Legal Memo. The particular components depend on what your court jurisdiction requires for briefs. My advice to you: Check your jurisdiction! State courts and Federal courts have certain rules for both the form and content of briefs. Within state and federal courts particular judges also have their own specific requirements. Before you file *anything ever* check local rules and the requirements of particular judges or judicial chambers.

Let's go over a basic template for your court briefings, this template is something that you can use as a starter for trial and appellate briefs, depending on local rules and requirements.

1. Sample Brief Container and Components

A legal brief generally contains some combination of these components:

    I.   Statement of the Issues

    II.   Statement of Facts

    III. Argument

    IV. Conclusion

To flesh out the components of a legal brief, I will use an example from a real federal case, *Chicago Lawyers' Committee v. Craigslist*, 519 F.3d 666, 2008 WL 681168 (2008). Below I will quote from the briefs of each side of the legal dispute.[1] The Chicago Lawyer's Committee for Civil Rights (CLC) sued Craigslist alleging housing discrimination in online advertising.

a.   Statement of the Issues

The issues in a persuasive brief are stated persuasively, not in an objective manner, as in a predictive or objective memo.

The CLC frames the Issue as follows:

> Whether § 230(c) of the Communications Decency Act immunizes Fair Housing Act violations by Internet Service Providers (ISPs) that make efforts to block and screen offensive discriminatory housing advertisements *and* by ISPs that fail to block and screen?[2]

Whereas Craigslist frames the Issue as follows:

> Whether Section 230 immunizes Craigslist, which is indisputably a "provider" of an "interactive computer

---

[1]   Excerpts from the *Craigslist* briefs provided with permission from Thomson Reuters.

[2]   *Chicago Lawyers' Committee For Civil Rights Under Law, Inc., Plaintiff-Appellant v. Craigslist Inc., Defendant-Appellee*, 2007 WL 3081735 (C.A.7).

service" within the meaning of the statute, from liability under the FHA for the allegedly unlawful content of website postings that indisputably were created entirely by third-party users of the Craigslist service.[3]

The Statement of the Case begins with a Statement of the **Theory of the Case.**

The Theory of the Case is your overarching conception of your case and the reason your client should prevail. In other words, it is the mental framework or umbrella that covers all the specific points, facts, and arguments. You should provide a clear view of what the case is about in your Theory of the Case.

A good Theory of the Case must do three things:

(1) Tell a compelling story;

(2) Be consistent with *all* of the facts at the various stages of the proceedings;

(3) Lead to the conclusion that you want the court to reach.

One way to construct your Theory of the Case is to begin this section with:

"This is a case about . . . ."

The Theory of the Case, however, is not a legal conclusion. For example, the Theory of the Case is not:

"Craigslist violated the Fair Housing Act."

Neither is the Theory of the Case a bunch of factual conclusions strung together:

---

[3] *Chicago Lawyers' Committee For Civil Rights Under Law, Inc., Plaintiff-Appellant v. Craigslist, Inc., Defendant-Appellee,* 2007 WL 4453962 (C.A.7), 2.

"The Fair Housing Act prevents discrimination in housing. Craigslist published housing advertisements. The advertisements violated the Fair Housing Act."

Finally, do not confuse your *Theory* of the Case with the *themes* of the case: Themes are factual characterizations that provide an emotional or moral resonance to your argument and that make your client more sympathetic and your opponent less sympathetic (we will discuss themes next in **Statement of Facts**).

Next, include an *abbreviated factual narrative* in your Statement of the Case. This narrative should follow the Theory of the Case in the same paragraph. The factual narrative should provide a brief summary of the relevant facts of your case, not every detailed fact that will be contained in the Statement of Facts.

Finally, provide the *procedural history* of the case. For example:

On February 3, 2006, CLC filed a one-count complaint, alleging that Craigslist violated the FHA by publishing discriminatory housing ads posted by third-party users on Craigslist's website. On April 14, 2007, Craigslist answered and simultaneously moved for judgment on the pleadings pursuant to Fed. R. Civ. P. 12(c), on the ground that Section 230 provides it with immunity from CLC's claim.

On November 14, 2006, the district court issued a Memorandum Opinion and Order granting Craigslist's motion, holding that Section 230 immunizes Craigslist from CLC's FHA claim. (A002-A029.) In its opinion, the court recognized that "near unanimous case law holds that Section 230(c) affords immunity" to service providers such as Craigslist from suits "that seek to hold [them] liable for third-party content." The district court declined to follow these precedents, concluding instead that Section 230(c)(1) bars only claims that "require, to establish liability, a finding that [the service provider] published third-party content." While the district court did not attempt to define the "full contours of the word 'publisher' or what constitutes 'treat[ment] as a publisher' " it nonetheless had little difficulty concluding that CLC's claim is barred even under its ostensibly more narrow construction: "[T]o hold [c]raigslist liable under [FHA] Section 3604(c) would be to treat [c]raigslist as if it were the publisher of third-party content" and therefore, "the plain language of Section 230(c)(1) forecloses CLC's cause of action."

On November 17, 2006, CLC moved to alter or amend the judgment pursuant to Fed. R. Civ. P. 59(e). CLC asserted that the district court had committed manifest error of law by holding that CLC had not stated a claim against Craigslist for "printing" the housing notices at issue, as supposedly distinct from CLC's claim against Craigslist for "publishing" the notices (and therefore supposedly not subject to 230 immunity as uniquely construed by the district court). The district court denied CLC's motion, holding that Craigslist did not "print" the housing notices at issue, "within any reasonable interpretation of that word, as defined when Congress enacted the FHA."[4]

b.   Statement of Facts

In a brief your goal is to be persuasive, not objective, as in the interoffice Memos we worked though in prior chapters. You should

---

[4] *Chicago Lawyers' Committee For Civil Rights Under Law, Inc., Plaintiff-Appellant v. Craigslist, Inc., Defendant-Appellee*, 2007 WL 4453962 (C.A.7), 2-3.

take the position most favorable to your client in explaining the facts relevant to the legal issues, without fabricating or creating additional facts.

Your Statement of Facts will follow the themes of your argument throughout the telling of your story. From your Statement of Facts, the reader will discern a roadmap to your legal argument.

For example, the CLC framed the Statement of Facts in its brief to tell the story of a large corporation that is violating the Fair Housing Act, as follows (citations in the original brief are omitted):

> CLC's mission is to promote and protect civil rights, particularly the civil rights of the poor, ethnic minorities, and disadvantaged. CLC strives to eliminate discriminatory housing practices by: (1) educating people about their rights under the fair housing and fair lending laws; (2) investigating complaints of fair housing discrimination; (3) providing referrals to other legal services organizations for non-discrimination housing matters; (4) advocating on a wide range of housing related issues, such as public housing, increased affordable housing, and fair and equal mortgage lending opportunities; and (5) providing free legal services to individuals and groups who wish to exercise their fair housing rights and secure equal housing opportunities.

> Craigslist operates an Internet website accessible at "chicago.craigslist.org," among other Internet addresses, that contains many types of advertisements, including those for the sale or rental of housing units. Housing advertisements are routinely posted on Craigslist's website, a large number of which indicate discriminatory housing preferences based on six protected classes: race, color, national origin, sex, religion, and familial status. To illustrate, discriminatory housing advertisements

posted on Craigslist's website have contained the following statements: "NO MINORITIES"; "Non-Women of Color NEED NOT APPLY"; "African Americans and Arabians tend to clash with me so that won't work out"; "Requirements: Clean Godly Christian Male"; "Only Muslims apply"; and "No children."

Craigslist allows housing providers to freely use its website to post discriminatory advertisements and to conceal their identities by assuming an anonymous email address with the domain name "craigslist.org." Craigslist acknowledges it has made no effort to block or screen discriminatory advertisements posted on its website.[5]

By contrast, Craigslist framed its Statement of Facts in its response brief as a small company working hard to provide extensive services:

With a staff of less than 30 people and a single office in California, Craigslist operates craigslist.org, a popular, fast-growing website dedicated to local community classifieds and forums, where people share ideas and find things they need or want in their lives, including jobs, dates, cars, activities, community information, and housing. The Craigslist service comprises classifieds and forums for 450 cities in the United States, including Chicago. The vast majority of Craigslist's services, including all portions of the site devoted to the Chicago community at issue in CLC's Complaint, are provided without charge.

The services offered on the craigslist.org website are divided into numerous categories, including community

---

[5] *Principal Brief of Chicago Lawyers' Committee for Civil Rights under Law, Chicago Lawyers' Committee For Civil Rights Under Law, Inc., Plaintiff-Appellant v. Craigslist Inc., Defendant-Appellee,* 2007 WL 3081735 (C.A.7).

announcements, for sale postings, upcoming event notices, personal ads, job postings, roommate ads, and notices for housing rentals and sales. Persons who visit craigslist.org (and select the city of their choice) and "click" on "housing" are presented with a choice of either posting a notice for housing or looking at housing notices posted by other users of the website. If a visitor indicates a desire to post a notice for housing (to sell, buy or rent housing or find a roommate), the website presents a series of choices for the category of notice the user seeks to post on the website (*e.g.*, "rooms & *4 shares," "room/share wanted," "apartments for rent," "apts wanted," "real estate for sale," and "real estate wanted"). After the visitor indicates the kind of notice he or she wishes to post, the website prompts him or her to fill in a number of relevant general "fields" (*e.g.*, rent or price, location, and contact information).

Throughout the "housing" pages, the website includes educational information regarding the fair housing laws and their laudable objectives and alerting users of the illegality of posting discriminatory ads.

The quantity of user-supplied information exchanged on craigslist.org is enormous: in a typical month in 2006, users post more than 10 million new notices to the site. CLC's own Brief estimates that "[w]ebsites like [c]raigslist receive literally millions of 'hits' and are viewed by thousands of people every day seeking to rent an apartment or buy a home." As of 2006, the number of classified ads that users post to craigslist.org was increasing at a rate of approximately one-hundred percent per year.[6]

In these contrasting Issue Statements, Statements of Facts, and theories of the case, you almost get the idea that there are completely different legal issues before the court. That differentiation is common and desirable, as the writer-advocate frames the facts to support the legal theory he or she hopes will prevail for the client in court.

c. Argument

Your legal argument in a brief may not be as religiously organized in the TREACC manner akin to the Discussion section in the objective Memo we discussed. In a brief, the framework exists, but may be a bit looser to provide for positioning of the argument.

Often in a brief we see a CRAC framework, or:

Conclusion

Rule

Application

Conclusion

Brief writers use the **RA** framework rather than a REA (Rule, Explanation and Application) framework that contains detailed fact comparisons.

For persuasive briefs, following CRAC means that you do not compare and contrast the facts of your client's case to the precedent you are citing for rules.

In briefing more complicated cases for argument, comparison to precedent case facts may not be either useful or required to support the legal point. Fact analogies and distinctions are not as

---

[6]   *Brief of Craigslist, Chicago Lawyers' Committee For Civil Rights Under Law, Inc., Plaintiff-Appellant v. Craigslist, Inc., Defendant-Appellee*, 2007 WL 4453962 (C.A.7), 3.

useful in a persuasive brief because (1) the facts of a precedent will rarely (if ever) be identical and can always be distinguished; and (2) your goal is for the court to follow the RULE you have stated (and not to follow a rule to an end that will hurt your client).

Rather, the argument is presented as streamlined, persuasive view of the legal issues to the court, and the argument may articulate an act or regulation as the "Rule," and the purpose and intent of the act or regulation as the Application.

In some briefs, the Conclusion (Thesis) may appear solely in the form of a heading (although I suggest that you repeat that Conclusion/Thesis heading in the first sentence of your argument. I call this the "echo method").

To illustrate the CRAC organization in an argument, I return to the Craigslist case. First, the CLC presents its argument from the perspective of unlawful discriminatory behavior prohibited by the Fair Housing Act:

I.   The Fair Housing Act Makes Newspapers And Their Online Counterparts Liable For Discriminatory Ads Written By Third Parties.

> This heading operates as a Conclusion or C in CRAC. I recommend that you **echo** the heading in the first sentence of the argument, providing a thesis conclusion within the argument text.

Nearly forty years after Congress passed the Fair Housing Act-to ensure equal access to housing regardless of one's race, color, national origin, gender, religion, and familial status-discrimination continues to be openly promoted throughout the Chicago housing market, as evidenced by the housing advertisements at issue in this case, advertisements that openly declare discriminatory preferences such as

"NO MINORITIES," "No children," and "African Americans and Arabians tend to clash with me so that won't work out."

> Emotional appeal in explaining the governing Act the FHA.

Discriminatory housing advertisements stigmatize and insult home-seekers, deter them from pursuing housing, mislead the public into thinking that it is acceptable to base housing decisions on factors such as race, gender, and family status, and deprive individuals of housing opportunities that they lawfully should enjoy.

The FHA condemns the making, printing, or publishing of discriminatory housing advertisements and declares equally offensive the causing or enabling of others to place such advertisements.

> RULE Focuses on the Fair Housing Act, and authority condemning discrimination in hiring. Explains the purpose of the FHA through precedent, not through case facts, though.

Congress passed the FHA to comprehensively "provide, within constitutional limitations, for fair housing throughout the United States." 42 U.S.C.A. § 3601 (2001). "The language of the Act is broad and inclusive," and reflects "a policy that Congress considered to be of the highest priority." *Trafficante v. Metro. Life Ins. Co.,* 409 U.S. 205, 209, 211 (1972). The FHA must be given a generous construction. *City of Edmonds v. Oxford House, Inc.*, 514 U.S. 725, 731 (1995). In § 3604(a) and (b), the FHA prohibits discrimination in the sale or rental of housing. The following subsection, (c), prohibits any sort of notice, statement, or advertisement that indicates a discriminatory preference or limitation based on various protected classes.

Section 3604(c) of the FHA makes it unlawful:

> Here, CLC cites a governing rule from the U.S. Code.

To make, print, or publish, or cause to be made, printed, or published any notice, statement, or advertisement, with respect to the sale or rental of a dwelling that indicates any preference, limitation, or discrimination based on race, color, religion, sex, handicap, familial status, or national origin, or an intention to make any such preference, limitation, or discrimination. 42 U.S.C.A. § 3604(c) (2001).

Congress gave § 3604(c) a remarkably expansive reach by making it applicable to housing providers who are exempt from other FHA provisions, by prohibiting statements that are unintentionally discriminatory, and extending coverage to newspapers and other communication outlets that print, publish or otherwise make public discriminatory preferences. *U.S. v. Hunter*, 459 F.2d 205, 211 (4th Cir. 1972) (holding that the "congressional prohibition of discriminatory advertisements was intended to apply to newspapers as well as *any other publishing medium*") (emphasis added); *Mayers v. Ridley*, 465 F.2d 630, 633 (D.C. Cir. 1972) (Wright, J., concurring) (concluding that the "proscription against 'publication' should therefore be read more broadly to bar *all devices for making public racial preferences in the sale [or rental] of real estate*") (emphasis added).

> The Explanation here is the purpose of the Regulation, rather than a case Explanation of Facts.

With the emergence of the Internet, everyday activities—such as reading the news, managing bank accounts, shopping for groceries, seeking employment or housing—are increasingly done online. Housing advertisements are now more commonly published on the Internet rather than in newspapers. Websites like Craigslist receive literally millions of "hits" and are viewed by thousands of people every day seeking to rent an apartment or buy a home. Sadly, housing discrimination has made its presence felt online. This case calls into question the extent to which (if at all) the FHA will remain an effective enforcement tool against discriminatory online housing advertisements.

> CLC buries the discussion of the applicability of the CDA.

To avoid FHA liability here, Craigslist asserts blanket immunity under § 230 of the CDA, thereby raising an important issue of statutory construction regarding the extent to which Congress protected ISPs from civil liability. The district court held that § 230's immunity protection is comprehensive as against all claims having "publication" as an element. We disagree and submit that this Court's opinion in *GTE*, and § 230's text, title, headings, structure, policy, and legislative history, compel a much different reading: one that provides no protection whatsoever to ISPs for information content of their own and no protection for offensive third-party content when the ISP makes no attempt to block and screen such content. Section 230 shields an ISP from civil liability for offensive third-party content only if the ISP undertakes, in good faith, to block or screen offensive, third-party material.[7]

> CLC's argument is pure policy, contrasting from our work in predictive memoranda, where we are comparing facts and the way the court applied the law to different facts.

Whereas, in the excerpt from the argument below, Craigslist argues from a regulatory perspective that it is immune from any liability for advertisements placed by third parties in its online forum. Craigslist supports its assertion entirely based on the CDA and controlling authority interpreting that CDA regulation:

> Conclusion/Thesis appears in the heading and focuses on the breadth of authority in support of Craigslist's position

I.   Courts Throughout the Country Have Uniformly Held That Section 230(c)(1) Provides Broad Immunity from Liability for Unlawful Third-Party Content.

The first operative provision of Section 230, § 230(c)(1), declares that "[n]o provider or user of an

---

[7]   *Chicago Lawyers' Committee For Civil Rights Under Law, Inc., Plaintiff-Appellant v. Craigslist Inc., Defendant-Appellee*, 2007 WL 3081735 (C.A.7).

interactive computer service shall be treated as the publisher or speaker of any information provided by another information content provider."

> Craigslist begins the argument by **echoing** the heading. Substantively, there is no discussion of the FHA at all. Craigslist relies on the immunity provided by the CDA and precedent interpreting that provision.

Over the past decade, courts deciding the meaning of this provision have uniformly held that it broadly immunizes online providers such as Craigslist from liability for dissemination of unlawful content that is created by others. This construction has been embraced by the federal courts of appeals for the First, Third, Fourth, Ninth and Tenth Circuits; by federal district courts in most if not all of the other Circuits (including the Seventh Circuit); by two State supreme courts; and by many other state courts.

> Craigslist piles on support with precedent authority from five federal circuit courts of appeals.

In the first case to consider Section 230(c)(1), *Zeran v. America Online, Inc.*, 129 F.3d 327, 330 (4th Cir. 1997), *cert. denied*, 524 U.S. 937 (1998), the Fourth Circuit (Wilkinson, C.J.) held that this provision "creates a federal immunity to *any cause of action* that would make service providers liable for information originating with a third-party user of the service." (Emphasis added.) Every other federal appellate court to decide what § 230(c)(1) means has agreed, recognizing that it creates a "robust" immunity that extends to all manner of content and claims. *See, e.g., Carafano v. Metrosplash.com, Inc.*, 339 F.3d 1119, 1123 (9th Cir. 2003) (observing that Ninth Circuit's first decision construing § 230(c)(1) (*Batzel v. Smith*, 333 F.3d 1018 (9th Cir. 2003), *cert. denied*, 541 U.S. 1085 (2004)) had "joined the consensus developing across other courts of appeal that § 230(c) provides broad immunity for publishing content provided primarily by third parties"); *see also, Universal Commc'n Sys., Inc. v. Lycos, Inc.*, 478 F.3d 413, 415 (1st Cir. 2007) ("In Section 230. . . Congress has granted broad immunity to entities. . . that facilitate the speech of others on the Internet."); *Green v. America Online, Inc.*, 318 F.3d 465, 471 (3d Cir. 2003) ("By its terms, § 230 provides immunity to AOL as a publisher or speaker of information originating from another information content provider"), *cert. denied*, 540 U.S. 877 (2003); *Ben Ezra, Weinstein & Co. v. America Online, Inc.*, 206 F.3d 980, 984-85 (10th Cir. 2000) (Section 230(c)(1) "creates a federal immunity to any state law cause of action that would hold computer service providers liable for information originating with a third-party"), *cert. denied*, 531 U.S. 824 (2000); *see also Noah v. AOL-Time Warner Inc.*, No. 03-1770, 2004 WL 602711 (4th Cir. Mar. 24, 2004) (*per curiam* affirmance of 261 F. Supp. 2d 532 (E.D. Va. 2003)) (holding that § 230(c)(1) immunized online provider from liability under Title II of the federal Civil Rights Act for users' messages that allegedly discriminated against Muslims).

Language "legions" indicates an enormous quantity of law in favor of Craigslist's position. The subsequent paragraphs explain or illustrate the supporting precedent.

Legions of federal district courts likewise have concluded that § 230(c)(1) broadly immunizes providers of interactive computer services from liability for disseminating allegedly unlawful third-party content. In fact, while the Seventh Circuit has yet to determine how § 230(c)(1) should be construed, three district court decisions in this circuit (including one from the Northern District of Illinois that preceded the decision on review here) adhered to the broad construction that has prevailed everywhere else. *See Morrison v. America Online, Inc.*, 153 F. Supp. 2d 930, 933-34 (N.D. Ind. 2001) (§ 230(c)(1) bars defamation claim against online service provider for allegedly defamatory emails authored by subscriber); *Does v. Franco Prods.*, Case No. 99-C-7885, 2000 WL 816779, at * 4 (N.D. Ill. Jun. 22, 2000) (§ 230(c)(1) "creates federal immunity against any state law cause of action that would hold computer service providers liable for information originating from a third party"), *aff'd on other grounds, Doe v. GTE Corp.*, 347 F.3d 655 (7th Cir. 2003); *see also Associated Bank-Corp. v. Earthlink, Inc.*, Case No. 05-C-0233-S, 2005 WL 2240952, at *4 (W.D. Wis. Sept. 13, 2005) ("Imposing liability on Defendant for the inaccurate information provided by a third-party content provider would treat Defendant as the publisher, a result § 230 specifically proscribes").

> After piling on the federal and state law precedent, Craigslist now provides support via legislative intent.

State trial and appellate courts, including two state supreme courts, have also consistently held that § 230(c)(1) is an independent immunity provision that protects online providers from liability for unlawful third-party content. *See Barrett v. Rosenthal*, 146 P.3d 510 (Cal. 2006); *Doe v. America Online, Inc.*, 783 So. 2d 1010, 1013-17 (Fla. 2001) ("*Florida Doe* ") (§ 230 immunizes online service provider from liability under state criminal statutes arising from allegedly harmful chat room messages originated by subscriber).

Significantly, Congress has explicitly endorsed the courts' consistent construction of § 230(c)(1) as an independent source of broad immunity by intentionally expanding Section 230's reach—as construed in *Zeran* and its progeny—into a new context. In 2002, Congress passed the "Dot Kids Implementation and Efficiency Act," establishing a new "kids.us" subdomain, dedicated to content deemed safe for minors, within the federally controlled ".us" Internet domain. *See* 47 U.S.C. § 941. In enacting that statute, Congress specifically extended the protections of Section 230 to cover certain entities that would operate in the new sub-domain, knowing full well how Section 230 had been applied in the courts. § 941(e)(1). The definitive committee report accompanying the new statute could not have been more clear and direct in embracing the way that courts had unanimously construed § 230(c)(1). Citing *Zeran, Ben Ezra*, and *Florida Doe* as key examples, the committee report declared that "[t]he courts have correctly interpreted section 230(c)," and that "[t]he Committee intends these interpretations of Section 230(c) to be equally applicable to those entities covered by [the new statute]." H.R. Rep. No. 107-449, at 13 (2002). In these circumstances, there can be no question that the consistent body of case law is correct.

This case is essentially the same as *Zeran, Lycos, Green, Carafano, Ben Ezra, Florida Doe* and the many other cases in which plaintiffs have sought to hold interactive computer service providers liable for unlawful content that originated from their users' content. Just as in each of those cases, Section 230 bars CLC's claim here.[8]

d.   Conclusion

In a persuasive brief, the Conclusion is very short and simple:

CONCLUSION

For the foregoing reasons, the Court should reverse the district court's grant of judgment on the pleadings and remand for further proceedings.

You will have exhausted all of your arguments in the body of your brief and the Conclusion is a formal bookend.

B.   Sample CRAC

Below is a **Sample CRAC** extracted from the CLC Brief. You will note that the recommended internal structure I recommend for the Application section of TREACC is contained here in the CRAC, albeit in a different order. The CRAC framework is a bit more flexible in that for persuasive purposes, the brief-writer will choose to emphasize different points:

(C) **[Conclusion on the issue]:** The Fair Housing Act makes newspapers and their online counterparts liable for discriminatory ads written by third parties. **[This Conclusion was provided in the Heading]**.

(R) Congress passed the FHA to comprehensively "provide, within constitutional limitations, for fair housing throughout the

[8]   *Chicago Lawyers' Committee For Civil Rights Under Law, Inc., Plaintiff-Appellant v. Craigslist, Inc., Defendant-Appellee,* 2007 WL 4453962 (C.A.7), 9-14.

United States." 42 U.S.C.A. § 3601 (2001). "The language of the Act is broad and inclusive," and reflects "a policy that Congress considered to be of the highest priority." *Trafficante v. Metro. Life Ins. Co.*, 409 U.S. 205, 209, 211 (1972). The FHA must be given a generous construction. *City of Edmonds v. Oxford House, Inc.*, 514 U.S. 725, 731 (1995). [**The Rules are all cited to the source, either statute or precedent**].

(A) [**Reviews opponent's flawed argument**]: To avoid FHA liability here, Craigslist asserts blanket immunity under § 230 of the CDA, thereby raising an important issue of statutory construction regarding the extent to which Congress protected ISPs from civil liability. [**Explanation of Applicable Rule**]: The district court held that § 230's immunity protection is comprehensive as against all claims having "publication" as an element. [**Conclusion on the Rule**]: We disagree and submit that this Court's opinion in GTE, and § 230's text, title, headings, structure, policy, and legislative history, compel a much different reading: one that provides no protection whatsoever to ISPs for information content of their own and no protection for offensive third-party content when the ISP makes no attempt to block and screen such content. [**Expand on supporting facts**]: Websites like Craigslist receive literally millions of "hits" and are viewed by thousands of people every day seeking to rent an apartment or buy a home. Sadly, housing discrimination has made its presence felt online.

(C) [**Conclusion on the issue**]: Section 230 shields an ISP from civil liability for offensive third-party content only if the ISP undertakes, in good faith, to block or screen offensive, third-party material.

> **Pro-Tip: Checklist for Brief Components**
>
> Use the checklist below to ensure that your brief includes all of the generally relevant sections and related substantive content. When filing a brief in court, be sure to consult the local rules for the brief requirements.

I. **Overview/Statement of the Case**

- Articulate the Theory of the Case
- Identify the parties
- Provide brief summary of facts
- Include procedural history

II. **Statement of Facts**

- Set forth the facts in a persuasive narrative
- Include all legally significant facts
- Include all relevant background facts
- Take a position in favor of your client and provide sympathetic value
- State facts accurately
- Include all facts that you use in the Argument section to illustrate rules
- Omit opinions and editorializing
- Include and downplay legally significant unfavorable facts

III. **Issue Statement**

- State the legal issue in the context of the client's facts

- If stated in question form, frame so as to suggest an affirmative answer

IV. Headings

- Headings and subheadings provide an outline of the Argument
- Headings are framed as legal assertions that are favorable to the client and are supported with legally relevant facts
- Headings address the Issue or Questions stated

V. Rules

- Synthesized rules are clearly and completely stated and cited to precedent authority
- Synthesized rules are framed favorably toward client and support legal conclusion

VI. Explanation

Rule Explanation of precedent authority illustrates the way the prior courts applied the synthesized rule to the facts in the precedent cases.

- Explanation includes Holdings, legally significant Facts, and Reasoning of the cases discussed (**FHR**)
- Facts from precedent cases included in the Explanation are related to/illustrative of the synthesized legal rules

VII. Argument: Application of Rule to Client's Facts

- Application of rule to client's facts illustrates the Theory of the Case
- Argument is organized into points and sub-points

- First sentence of the Argument should echo the point heading

- **Points and sub-points follow the CRAC or CRACC paradigm:**

    Conclusion

    Rule Synthesis + Explanation

    Application of Rule to Facts

    Counterargument (if any)

    Conclusion

VIII. Counterargument

- Counterargument provides an alternative argument and rebuts the arguments raised by the opponent

IX. Organization

- **Transitions** between paragraphs are clear

- Sentences within a paragraph relate to one another coherently and flow together

X. Proofreading

- All sentences are checked for correct grammar, spelling, and citation form

PART V

Legal Writing Quick Tips

There may not be any real shortcuts to great legal writing, because you have to commit the time and practice to perfect your craft. You can take numerous steps both to simplify and streamline your writing process, however. Your habits of writing and of mind will help you focus and produce your best work both in law school, and as a practicing attorney.

CHAPTER 9

Writing Under Pressure

All of these happy examples seem like a fun way to spend your day (and they are), but the reality is you will not always have all day to construct your legal analyses either when you are drafting writing assignments in law school or when you are practicing law. The truth is attorneys lead very busy lives and have to balance many different professional and personal obligations.

To that extent, this chapter provides some advice for managing your time.

A. First Year Tips

You will read a lot of precedent cases. Try to be as efficient as possible:

1. Read Cases for Structure First, Then Read for Content

1. I suggest that you read the **Holding first.**

    Q: Why should you read the Holding first?

> A: You should read the Holding first so you know how the court decided the case. You will find out immediately if the decision is helpful or hurtful to your client's position in your memo or brief.

2.   If the Holding appears helpful, go back to the beginning of the opinion and **read the opinion for structure.**

> Q: What does it mean to read for structure?

> A: Reading for structure means taking note the following:

> - Where does the opinion begin?

> - What sections address the legal points you are looking for?

> Q: Is this method tedious?

> A: Yes, yes this method is tedious.

> Q: Will this method enhance your original understanding and expedite your classification of important and unimportant material?

> A: Yes, yes this tedious method will help you classify important material.

3.   Adopt a *meta* understanding of precedent cases: Precedent is the result of courts applying a statute or common law in a particular jurisdiction to a set of facts argument presented by an attorney in a filed lawsuit.

> - Precedent is set by courts for each state at every level

> - Precedent is set by federal courts at the trial, appellate, and Supreme Court levels.

4. Hone in on the most important part of the precedent.

    Q: What is the most important part of a particular precedent?

    A: It depends! (Don't hate me!)

        The answer depends on what legal support you are looking for in the precedent to support the analysis in your brief or memo.

        But generally you want to focus on the Facts, Holding, and Reasoning (the **FHR**).

5. Precedent is key!

    Q: When you need precedent cases?

    A: Always! You always need precedent as authority to support your analysis in all legal documents, for example:

    *   Memos
    *   Email
    *   Client and opposing counsel correspondence
    *   Persuasive briefs

6. Read the Statutes!

    Q: How do you read a Statute? Statutes are difficult to read!

    A: Do not try to understand a Statute at your first reading. Remember that the legislatures draft Statutes as a reflection of the compromise of constituencies resulting in law that is not always (rarely is) clearly written for an easy understanding.

Read a Statute one sentence at a time sentence and pay attention to the punctuation. For example, note when a Statute uses *and* and when it uses *or*.

2. *Organizing Strategies*

Getting started on your analytical writing is harder than the actual writing. I can think of 25 things I can do to procrastinate getting started on my writing.[1] Do not do those things. Get started. Do those other things later; you are under deadline pressure.

a. Outlining

Everyone is probably telling you to outline your writing and everything else. You should do that. Is there such thing as a perfect outline? No, there is not. Outlining can mean as little as jotting down your organization in single words to fleshing out your ideas in complete sentences. Eventually you will write those complete sentences; just get started in the easiest way you can.

b. Tools

To begin, have a battery of tools at the ready, including:

- Legal Note Pads
- Index Cards
- Sticky-Notes
- Pens
- Colored Highlighters
- Pencils
- A Ruler

---

[1]   If you are going to procrastinate, which I do not recommend, try employing a Productive Procrastination Program (PPP) to get everything else done in your life and you household before you start your writing.

If this sounds like your pencil box for elementary school, it is. It is proven that it is better to write your thoughts than to type them.

c.   Substance

Now for the substance:

Summarize the legal Issue(s)

What are the Facts? What do I do with the Facts?

- Organize your Facts chronologically

- Associate the appropriate Facts with the corresponding arguments

Q: Are all the Facts relevant?

A: No! The Facts that are relevant are the Facts that are *legally relevant* or relevant to the resolution of the legal issue. Including Facts that are not legally relevant will just distract your reader and throw the reader off track into never-never land, as in: "never, never gonna be able to figure out what you are talking about."[2]

d.   Authority

Choose your authority carefully using only relevant precedent. This book does not thoroughly cover legal research methods, but if you are doing your own research, and using online platforms, narrow your search terms.

e.   Discussion/Arguments

In a predictive memo, you will generally organize your discussion according to the order of the elements of the common law or statute relevant to your analysis as provided in the statute, common law, or by your professor.

---

[2]   Thanks to Jonathan Kirschmeier for this pointed quote.

In a persuasive brief you will probably want organize your Argument by placing your strongest arguments first.

f.   **Manage Stress**

I am not going to lie to you; law school and law practice is stress inducing. That is why it is important that you exercise self-care throughout your legal life.

First: BREATHE!

When you first receive an assignment do the exact opposite of what everyone else does and do not open the assignment. Just sit back for a second and collect your thoughts while you take five to six deeps breaths. When you are sufficiently peaceful, proceed to open your assignment packet.

Second: Don't Fuss Over Fancy Language

You may not know the perfect ten-dollar word to summarize your argument. Don't waste three hours pondering and searching for that word. The best legal analysis is communicated in simple words, organized in the most efficient manner, to make a clear, strong point.

Third: Keep Writing!

If you get stuck in one section of your assignment while writing under time constraints make sure to keep writing. Move to another section and keep going. Something you write in another section may trigger that inspiration you were seeking in the previous section and you can always go back.

Pro-Tip: Sports Analogies Extras!

Sitting in a timed writing assignment or exam and trying to figure out the perfect word or sentence is like hitting a tap in putt with the back of your putter blindfolded because you think there is no possible way you can miss, and when you miss the rest of the day is ruined just like the rest of your writing assignment is ruined by wasting your time.

Or, trying to figure out the perfect word in a timed writing assignment is like trying to shoot a free throw shot, one-handed in basketball; most of the time you are going to miss, and it's going to take longer for you to get right, whereas if you used two hands, you would have scored and moved on.

CHAPTER 10

Professor's Pet Peeves: Grammar and Structure

Your professor or employer will likely have some pet peeves for your written work product. You should pay very close attention to your professor or employer's preferences and rectify any language or grammar issues that may cause your professor to cringe. Ask them if they have a list of pet peeves.

The following is my list of pet peeves for grammar and sentence construction in legal writing.

1. Passive Voice

Please avoid passive voice in legal writing. Legal readers really appreciate active voice in almost most instances. Passive voice usually indicates vagueness or confusion over the subject, *i.e.*, who performed or acted in a particular action.

Here are some examples of passive sentence construction:

"The carpet **was removed** after the flood,"

As written, the above sentence does not reveal the subject or who (the actor) removed the carpet. An active construction, *i.e.*,

"Esmerelda removed the carpet after the flood," provides a specific context or subject in the sentence.

Also, when you write in passive voice, you invariably include extra words in the text. Try to avoid extra words when subject to a word count (as you will be for most, if not all, court-filed documents).

For example,

"The defendant was not the owner of the gun,"

has two more words than

"The defendant did not own the gun."

To check for passive voice, use the **Zombies Rule:**

If you add "by zombies" after the verb and the sentence sounds fine, the sentence is written in passive voice.

For example:

"My neighbor was eaten **by zombies**"

is passive, while

"Penelope ate **by zombies** my neighbor"

is not passive. If you remove **by zombies** from the second sentence you have active voice.

Test your sentences for the zombies and destroy the zombie's brain.

Another way to check for passive voice is to conduct a search of your word-processed document by highlighting the following words and combination of words throughout your legal analysis:

- was
- has
- has been
- have been

If you include a lot of these words individually or in combination within your legal analyses, chances are you are writing in passive voice.

2. That/Which

Nearly every legal writer is tempted to use "which" instead of "that" in their legal writing. My advice is that you **"which hunt"** in your written work.[1] The word "which" should be used sparingly and only after a comma. Do not be a "that" bigot.[2]

For example: "the dog which bit me was very scary" is improper. The sentence should be either:

"The dog that bit me was very scary," or

"The dog, which bit me, was very scary."

The important thing to remember is that a comma is required before the word "which," but that a comma is not required before the word "that." For the most part, try to eliminate the "which" in your writing and replace which with "that."[3]

3. That/Who-Whom

That refers to things, while who or whom refers to people. For example, "the dog **that** bit me was very large" is correct. "The students **that** were studying in the library" is improper because "students" refers to people; "the students **who were** studying the library" is the correct phrasing.

---

[1] See Bryan Garner, The Redbook: A Manual on Legal Style, 4th Ed. 2018.
[2] Yeah, this was Garner's idea, too. I agree with him.
[3] See The American Heritage Dictionary of the English Language, Fifth Ed. 2018, Houghton Mifflin Harcourt Pub. Co.

4. *Floating Quotations*

Many legal writers are tempted to start paragraphs with floating quotations in their written communication.

> "Floating quotations are entire sentences that appear within quotations marks, as complete sentences."

Your writing should introduce the source of the quotation whether the source is primary (from precedent) or secondary (from a law review article, for example). The reader should be able to tell from your writing, not from reading footnotes or a citation, whether you are quoting a primary source or a secondary source.

To ground a floating quotation, when quoting a source, introduce the quote with a **speaker tag**, such as: Professor Borman identifies, "floating quotations [as] entire sentences that appear within quotations marks. . . ." Or, you might say that "Floating quotations," according to Professor Borman, "confuse the reader."

5. *Block Quotations*

Block quotations are usually a serious pet peeve for the professor. First, when a busy legal reader sees a block quote, the reader becomes immediately irritated, and skips over the block quote. Second, only rarely does the block quotation provide the support the writer intends for his or her proposition.

Anytime you provide a quote you should introduce it and explain what the quote means, *i.e.*, summarize the quote first:

> "Justice Black explained the importance of determining wherein fault lay in a car accident as follows: . . ."

Do not rely on long quotations to convey your meaning without an introduction. The best way to make your interpretation clear is to break up the quotation into little pieces and explain each piece, tying them all together into one whole thought.

Make a point yourself, explain the meaning of your point in your own words, and then provide authority in support of your point in the form of a short quotation.

6. Paragraphs

Use many separate paragraphs in your legal writing, rather than single page or three-quarters long scary monster paragraphs. Smaller paragraphs are easier to read and convey the steps of your analysis or argument better than long, monster paragraphs. For example, the discussion of the different elements of a legal rule should be separated by paragraphs. Discussion of different precedent should be separated by paragraphs. Always use separate paragraphs to discuss the distinct issues or elements of a claim. Separate paragraphs are easier to read and demonstrate that you understand how to separate different discussion points.

7. Punctuation Belongs Inside Quotes

When you are using material that is contained in quotes the punctuation, as in a period or a comma, belongs inside the quotes.

For example, punctuate this way:

"Professor Borman provides great writing advice."

Not this way:

"Professor Borman provides great writing advice".

No, no, no, no. The period belongs INSIDE quote marks!

8. *The Court and Corporate Entities Are Not Human*

The courts and corporate entities should not be referred to as "they," or other human referential pronouns. Do not write "the court thought. . ." or "the company felt. . . ." Entities such as corporations, states, governments, counties, courts, regions, schools, and departments are not considered human for the purpose and in the context of legal writing.

If you find yourself writing that kind of sentence, stop and refer to the court or a company as "it." And then go back and rewrite the sentence again to omit the "it."

For example, convert this faulty construction:

"The court held that the owner was liable to the plaintiff for the dog bite. **They** held that the owner should have kept the dog on a leash"

To:

"The court held that the owner was liable to the plaintiff for the dog bite. The owner should have kept the dog on a leash."

9. *Commas*

When writing a list of items separated by commas in a series, use the **Oxford Comma.**

The Oxford Comma requires that when you are writing a list of single items, all items have a comma attached before the final item and the word "and." For example:

"My dining room table is covered with books, papers, and dirty dishes."

When you have items in a list that are longer than one word, you should substitute semicolons for the commas, particularly when the individual elements of the series are long and contain commas themselves.

For example:

> To establish a claim for intentional infliction of emotional distress, a plaintiff must show that: (1) the defendant acted intentionally or recklessly, both in doing the act and producing emotional distress; (2) the conduct was so outrageous in character and extreme in degree as to go beyond all bounds of decency; (3) the defendant's actions were the proximate cause of the emotional distress; and (4) the distress suffered was so severe that no reasonable person could be expected to endure it. *Buckley v. Trenton Sav. Fund Soc'y*, 111 N.J. 355, 366, 544. A.2d 857 (1988).

10. Ellipses

Use an ellipsis when you cut words out of a quotation. If you omit words from quoted material in the middle of a sentence, . . . use three periods with a space in between each period.

11. Verb Tense

When you are discussing the facts of a precedent case always use past tense: "The court held that the owner of the rabid dog was negligent." When you are discussing *your client's* case facts, use present or past tense, but not passive voice.

12. Spell-Checking

Spelling is the easiest error to fix and the most readily apparent error to the legal reader. Try to finish your written work far enough in advance to catch all misspelled words (because spellcheck programs will not catch all of them, *See, e.g.,* "statute" vs. "statue;" the former is not programmed into Microsoft Word).

13. Colloquial Language

Although in written legal communication we want to avoid archaic legalese, we do not want to take legal writing all the way to everyday colloquial language, dude. Proofread your writing for casual, conversational language. Law communication requires traditional formality and clear and concise writing.

14. Always Include a Subject After the Word "This"

My students will tell you that they often saw this comment in the margin of their writing: "This what?" I use a symbol to designate "this what" in the text of student writing after the word "this" if the word "this" is not followed by a subject: [-]

For example:

"This was very tall and constituted a spite fence under the statute."

This what?

"This *row of trees* was very tall and thus a spite fence under the statute."[4]

Yes:

In light of this *precedent*, ...

No:

In light of this, ...

---

[4]   Also avoid the overused word "constituted."

15. Tense

When you are discussing the facts of a precedent case always use past tense: "The court held that the owner of the rabid dog was negligent." When you are discussing *your client's* case, use present or past tense, but not passive voice.

16. No Court-Speak

The instant case is archaic court-speak and should never be used in your memos and briefs.

The case at hand is also archaic court-speak. The court has a case "at hand," because the court is deciding the case on its docket. Litigants should never use "the case at hand."

17. No Legalese

Avoid these phrases:

- Assuming arguendo
- *To wit*
- Whereas
- The aforementioned
- Hereinafter

18. Obviously, Clearly, and Other Intensifiers

These adverbs are intensifiers that inject your personal thought and opinion into your objective writing. Avoid these words.

Fun fact: the second your legal reader sees the word "clearly," he or she assumes the Statement, Conclusion, or Fact is *not* clear.

19. Pronouns

Use parties' names or legal position. Avoid he, she, her, him, even if it means you are repeating the name over and over again. Caveat: it is okay to use one pronoun in a sentence if you previously included the name in the same sentence.

20. I, We Statements (First Person/Third Party)

Do not insert yourself into the communication or the proceedings, by announcing "I believe. . . ." Stay remote. The legal reader is concerned about the analysis based on the precedent authority, not your personal opinion.

21. Since vs. Because

Since = time

Because = reason

"It has been *three hours* **since** I ate that chocolate bar."

"I am eating more chocolate now **because** *I am hungry.*"

22. Long Sentences

Sentences should not be longer than 25 words. Use a period to end your thought and start a new sentence. Avoid extending the length of a sentence with multiple, additional clauses and commas.

23. Finding and Holding

Trial courts are the finders of fact.

When discussing the actions of the trial court use **find** when referring to findings of fact and **rule** when referring to legal determinations.

Appellate courts are courts of *review*. Appellate courts review rulings and make legal determinations in the form of **holdings.**

When you are using appellate precedent as authority (you will almost always be using appellate precedent as authority) remember to write that the court *held* not *ruled.*

24. Party Names: Be Consistent

Use party names (last names).

Use party roles (home seller/home buyer).

Do not use plaintiff and defendant, as these terms do not permit the reader to fully understand the parties' relationship to each other *vis-à-vis* the facts.

In a single memo or brief, do not alternatively refer to a party as "The Handyman," then "Smith," and then "Mr. Smith."

25. Oh, Boy, Nominalizations Are So Wordy!

Compare:

"The sellers made a decision to accept the buyer's offer, so they issued an authorization to their broker to make an announcement of their decision."

To:

"The sellers decided to accept the buyer's offer, so they authorized their broker to announce their decision."

26. Avoid Throat-Clearing Phrases

Don't use any of these unnecessary introductory phrases:

- It is interesting to note that . . ."
- "It is important to note that . . ."
- "We can observe that. . . ."

- "As noted above . . ."
- "I believe . . ."

27. Simplify

Avoid wordiness! Eliminate phrases that can be replaced by a single word.

- At the time when = when
- At the point in time when = when
- As a result of = because
- By reason of the fact that = because
- Due to the fact that = because
- For the purpose of = to
- That was a case where = where

28. No Contractions

Although I use contractions generously throughout this book, do not (see what I did there?) use them in your legal analytical writing.

- Can't = cannot
- Don't = do not
- Won't = will not

CHAPTER 11

A Short & Happy Research Primer

We already covered quite a bit here about objective and persuasive writing and constructing your legal analysis. But what about researching your own authority? Your professor, your librarian, and your Westlaw representative will teach you research in depth but I'll provide a few tips here to get you started.

A. Basic Research Strategy

Legal research can be overwhelming. You need to organize your thoughts and your data before you start your research to be efficient.

1. Begin with Secondary Sources

When you are getting started on a legal research project, it is best to start with secondary sources. Remember secondary sources? We discussed secondary authority way back in Chapter 3.

A secondary source is any information that explains, clarifies, interprets, defines or assists you in understanding a particular legal topic. Secondary sources are encyclopedias law review articles, treatises, or hornbooks.

Secondary sources provide the big picture of your legal issue. Through secondary sources, you become familiar with the legal topic you need to research, frame the issues, and identify the applicable law. Secondary sources provide current information on your topic and also introduce you to "terms of art," or phrases you may not hear outside of that particular area of the law.

You should begin your research with secondary sources to help you find primary authority (precedent) material. Secondary sources contain citations to primary sources (precedent, statutes, and regulations) that will be useful to your resolution of the legal issue.

a.   Where Do I Start?

First, analyze your fact pattern or client's facts and determine your primary and any ancillary issues.

Then, first on paper, generate a list of key words and concepts. If you are not familiar with the area of law you are researching, begin to search secondary sources to obtain an understanding of the subject. Through secondary sources you can fine citation to primary authority.

On Westlaw[1] you search secondary sources this way:

Once you find primary authority (precedent), read and evaluate the authority.

b.   Depth of Treatment

The type of secondary source you use will depend on the depth of treatment you need to use to expand your knowledge of the law.

Treatises, Loose-leaf Services, and Practice Guides provide the most thorough information about your topic. Treatises provide in-depth treatment of single subject. Treatises may be a single volume or multi-volume and contain citations to primary and secondary authorities. In multi-volume treatises, you use the index found in the last volume of the set or the table of contents to find relevant sections in main volumes. In a hard copy, multi-volume treatise, check pocket parts for most recent case precedent.

---

[1]   All screenshots from Westlaw are used with generous permission from Thomson Reuters.

A treatise example in Westlaw:

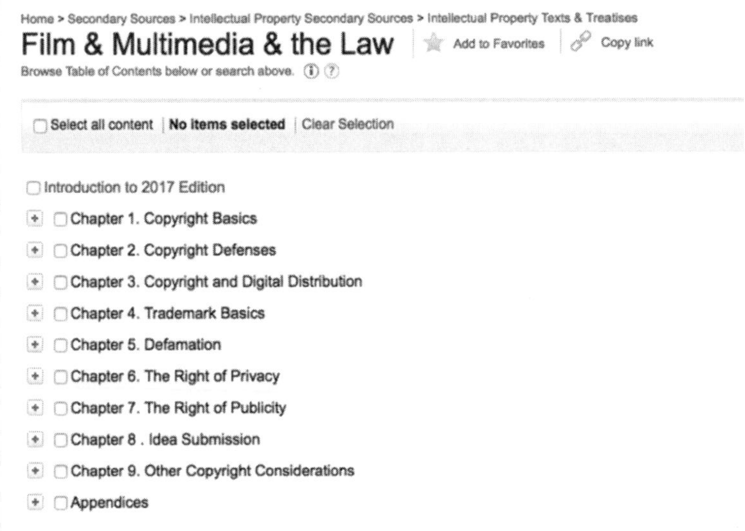
Home > Secondary Sources > Intellectual Property Secondary Sources > Intellectual Property Texts & Treatises
Film & Multimedia & the Law
Add to Favorites
Copy link
Browse Table of Contents below or search above.
Select all content
No items selected
Clear Selection
Introduction to 2017 Edition
Chapter 1. Copyright Basics
Chapter 2. Copyright Defenses
Chapter 3. Copyright and Digital Distribution
Chapter 4. Trademark Basics
Chapter 5. Defamation
Chapter 6. The Right of Privacy
Chapter 7. The Right of Publicity
Chapter 8 . Idea Submission
Chapter 9. Other Copyright Considerations
Appendices

Loose-leaf services are either single volume or multi-volume "mini-libraries" on specific topics. Loose-leaf services are updated through interfiling rather than pocket parts.

In Westlaw, you will find all of these resources here:

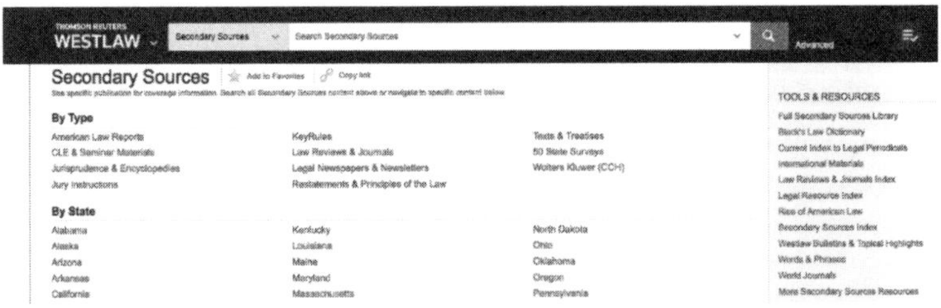
WESTLAW
Secondary Sources
By Type
American Law Reports
CLE & Seminar Materials
Jurisprudence & Encyclopedias
Jury Instructions
KeyRules
Law Reviews & Journals
Legal Newspapers & Newsletters
Restatements & Principles of the Law
Texts & Treatises
50 State Surveys
Wolters Kluwer (CCH)
By State
Alabama
Alaska
Arizona
Arkansas
California
Kentucky
Louisiana
Maine
Maryland
Massachusetts
North Dakota
Ohio
Oklahoma
Oregon
Pennsylvania
TOOLS & RESOURCES

Encyclopedias and Legal Periodicals provide more general information on a broad range of topics. Legal Encyclopedias provided easy to read explanations of legal concepts. Encyclopedias will point to cases, statutes or law review articles on the topic of

your research. National Encyclopedias include American Jurisprudence 2d (Am.Jur.) and Corpus Juris Secundum (CJS).

A Litigation Encyclopedia such as AmJur Proof of Facts contains a plethora of information to help with a trial, including summaries of the relevant law, elements to be proven for claims, which party has the burden of proof, considerations for defending a claim, checklists to help you organize, and sample depositions.

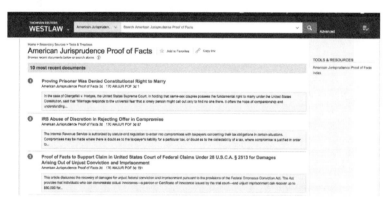

Encyclopedias are also available in your school library and public law libraries in old-school print form. To use print encyclopedias, look in the General Index at the end of a set of encyclopedias for your research topic. Find that topic and then the section in the corresponding volume. Use Table of Contents at beginning of each section to hone in on your topic.

Finally, dictionaries, Nutshells, and hornbooks are helpful in providing general background on a legal topic. Nutshells are abbreviated, concise treatises on specific topics, like a simplified hornbook, Nutshells are written by experts in the field and available as smaller, paperback books. Often you will find a Nutshell that corresponds specifically to a textbook you have in one of your law-topic courses.

Hornbooks are single-volume treatises that summarize general principles of specific area of law. Hornbooks discuss the most important cases on a particular legal topic. Hornbooks are organized in an outline form similar to the way your topical courses are organized.

Periodicals such as law reviews are also excellent secondary sources for your research. Law review articles provide scholarly, critical analysis of topical issues, provide recommendations for changes in the law, and citations to primary authority.

One great way to find law review articles is HeinOnline. HeinOnline provides access to .pdf copies of law review articles from every issue of almost every major journal.

Legal Newsletters are also a good research resource. Generally, practice-oriented and non-scholarly, legal newsletters are published by professional organizations such as the American Bar Association as well as local, state, and county bar associations.

The American Law Reports (ALRs) are annotated encyclopedic essays with commentary on legal issues. ALRs collect cases on a particular legal topic and provide in-depth treatment and cross-references to other sources.

For statutory research, look to annotated statutes. You will find annotated statutes for both state and federal statutes. Here is the United States Code Annotated (USCA) on Westlaw:

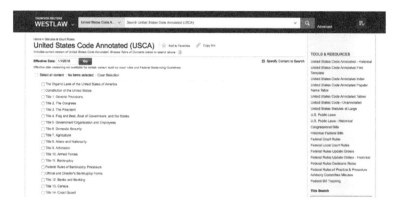

And here is an example of a state statute index:

How would you find an Illinois statute that includes the terms "Easter bunny" and "Santa Claus?"

Start in Illinois:

Use the search term "Easter bunny"

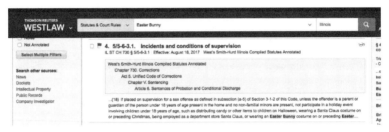

Click on that statute to see what why the flag is red.[2]

Many of the above resources are available free in your library in book form. There are also a number of free online resources, including the Social Science Research Network (SSRN), on online repository of scholarly works that includes article drafts, working papers, and final versions of articles. You can search SSRN by Title, Abstract, Keywords. SSRN articles are great for locating the most current commentary and analysis on "hot" legal topics.

Another great free resource online is Google Scholar. http://scholar.google.com/. Google Scholar is searchable by case name, article, and statute. You can restrict your Google Scholar searches by date.

c.   Common Question on Using Secondary Sources

Q: How do I know when to stop researching?

A: When you continue to see the same authority, precedent or answer over and over your research is complete.

---

[2]   The statute was amended to strike out some provisions and add new provisions and conditions. The portion about the Easter bunny is unchanged.

2. Finding Precedent (Case Law)

To locate the precedent, you find from using your secondary sources, you can search by Keyword and by using the Topic and Key Number (Digest) System on Westlaw.

Westlaw's Key Number System is organized alphabetically by subject matter and grouped by number. Key Numbers will help you refine your search.

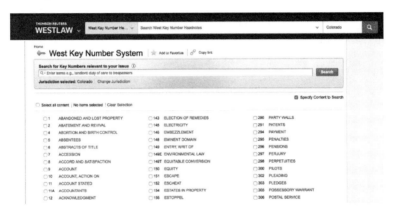

You will find the Key numbers in the Headnotes for each case precedent.

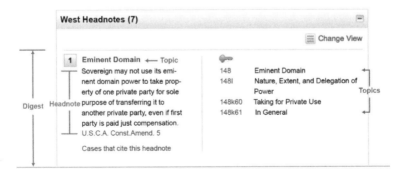

Read the synopsis to see if the precedent case is helpful:

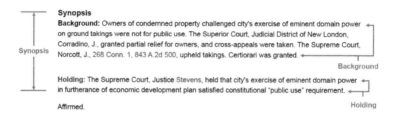

Use the Advanced Search feature in the top right corner to narrow your search results.

Once you are into the Advanced Search Page, use term connectors and expanders, featured on the side of the page, to construct a refined search. Terms and connectors such as: and, or, /s [within sentence], /p [within paragraph], /10 [within 10 words] will significantly refine your search.

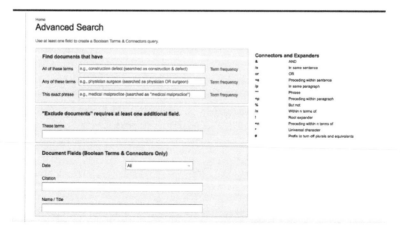

a. One Good Case Method

Every law school and research librarian recommend using the "one good case" method. The one good case method of legal research will help you build your research from one case you know is on point to your topic to find additional cases directly related to your topic. You can use the one good case method both online and with print resources to find relevant cases.

b. How Do You Identify That "One Good Case?"

You may already have one good case as a starting point in your assignment from your professor or your office supervisor.

If Not, **Ask**: When you work as a research assistant in law school or if you are working in a law office, ask the professor or the supervising attorney if there is one good case recommended as a starting point.

Use **Secondary Sources**: Remember to begin your research on a new legal issue by searching secondary sources, as described above.

Use **Annotated Statutes**: If a statute controls your legal question, find the statute in an annotated state or federal code that lists the precedent cases interpreting your legal question after the statute or code. Read through the case listings to find one good case.

Use **Digests**: Read the one good case in a West Reporter (book) or online. Review the headnotes to identify Key Numbers relevant to your issue and to find more relevant cases. In print, use the digest of the jurisdiction that is mandatory authority for your legal issue. Even if the one good case you find is from a state other than your jurisdiction, you can use the topic and key number in any state digest; the same topics and Key Numbers are used in every digest.

On **Westlaw** online, find your one good case through headnotes. Use KeyCite Notes to search links to the various categories of authorities that cite your case. Find the relevant Key Number and build a search, adding your preferred jurisdiction, date, and additional key words.

KeyCite: Find your one good case using KeyCite (described below) and you will retrieve links to additional cases that cite to your case. In addition to cases, KeyCite also lists statutes, administrative decisions, and secondary sources that cite your one good case, giving you a broader base of relevant authorities for your research.

c.   Citators: Ensure Good Law

Citators are services that list the cases and secondary resources that cite earlier cases and alert you to the status of the case. Use citators to see whether a case, statute, federal regulation, is "good law" (citing for validation) or to locate additional relevant authorities (citing for research).

Here's a little history for you that will explain why everyone calls checking citations "Shepardizing," no matter what method is used to check the citation: The name Shepards is derived from a legal service begun by Frank Shepard (1848–1902) in 1873:

> Shepard began publishing lists of cases in a series of books indexed to different jurisdictions. The citations were printed on gummed, perforated sheets, which could be divided and pasted onto pages of case law. Known as 'stickers,' these were literally torn to bits and stuck to pertinent margins of case reporters. By the early 20th century, the Frank Shepard Company was binding the citations into maroon volumes with "Shepard's Citations"

stamped in gold on their spines, much like the ones still found on library shelves.[3]

West uses a citator system called KeyCite. KeyCite editors review cases, statutes, regulations, administrative decisions, patents and trademarks.

At the top of the document a KeyCite flag tells you the status of a case, statute, regulation, administrative decision, patent or trademark, *i.e.*, whether the case is no longer good law (red flag), has negative treatment in subsequent cases (yellow flag), or has been appealed to the U.S. court of Appeals or the U.S. Supreme Court (blue and white flag).

The KeyCite Citing Reference tab shows how other authorities have interpreted that document so you can see the depth of the discussion and the topics discussed in the citing case.

Depth-of-Treatment Bars show you how extensively a cited case or administrative decision has been discussed by the citing case.

Quotation Marks indicate that the citing document directly quotes the cited case or administrative decision. Headnotes indicate which point of law the citing document discussed.

---

[3] Morris, Jane W. (May 2004). "The Future of Shepard's Citations in Print" (PDF). The Newsletter on the Committee of Relations with Information Vendors. American Association of Law Librarians. 26 (3): 3.

KeyCite®

KeyCite is the powerful citation research service available exclusively on Westlaw. Use KeyCite at every step of your research to help you find, understand, and update the law.

The KeyCite citation network is integrated with the West Key Number system. This integration allows KeyCite to connect documents that discuss the same legal issues with the analytical materials that explain those issues.

Once you have found a document upon which to base your legal argument, KeyCite Flags alert you to negative references or events that may impact the validity of that document.

• Cases & Administrative Decisions - some negative treatment, but not reversed or overruled
• Statutes & Regulations - proposed legislation or rule available, court decision has questioned validity, or prior version received negative treatment from a court
• Patents & Trademarks - not infringed, but did not rule on its validity, all or part valid and not infringed, held a trademark was not diluted, or held a trademark was not violated by unfair competition

• Cases & Administrative Decisions - no longer good for at least one point of law
• Statutes & Regulations - amended, repealed, superseded, or held unconstitutional or preempted in whole or in part
• Patents & Trademarks - all or part is invalid, invalid and not infringed, all or part of a patent is unenforceable due to the patentee's inequitable conduct, or a trademark is cancelled

A blue-striped flag indicates a document has been appealed to the U.S. Courts of Appeals or the U.S. Supreme Court (excluding appeals originating from agencies).

d.   Research Review

- Start with background research on for secondary sources on Westlaw or Google Scholar

- On Westlaw, search by Key word

- Remember to Focus on legal issues, not facts

- Use Topic and Key Number System

- Find topic and key number in secondary sources

- One Good Case method

- Make sure you have good law by using KeyCite

Final Thoughts on Legal Writing

The practice of law is perhaps the most rewarding work of any professional career. Cultivating an expertise on written legal analysis is not a fast process, but once you have the analytical thought process down your legal writing will become clear, organized, and persuasive.

Excellent legal writing is both a privilege and an art. Being able to craft concise and clear written, legal communication is a privilege because you are a small minority of professionals who learn to take on other people's legal issues and larger societal problems with the goal of resolution. Excellent legal writing is tremendously difficult to cultivate and is truly an art when achieve. Written legal analysis, as noted in the introduction and first chapters of this book, is the foundation of our country. When you draft a comprehensible and clear legal analysis on behalf of a client you are contributing to the resolution of problems, small and large, and to written legal history.

You cannot become a lawyer in an afternoon. Learning to practice law requires sustained effort and repetition of reasoning exercises reduced to writing.

To reason and write like a lawyer you need to perfect the following skills:

Think clearly using deductive processes to arrive at a conclusion, checking whether all of the required elements are present.

Identify the legal question to be answered and the rule that applies.

Identify ancillary questions and the sub-rules that apply: what is the logical order in which to answer the legal questions?

Avoid assumptions. Does anyone (everyone) know this one? When you assume "you make an ass of me."

Accept the fact that legal reasoning will not always produce binary (yes/no/right/wrong) answers. Correct answer is not always black and white; seek a *good* answer.

Understand both sides of the argument. A good lawyer knows the argument for both sides. In this class, you will research both sides of an issue and will not be tied to one position. You will always need to know the strong and weak arguments in favor and against your client. It is only by understanding the weaknesses of your argument that you can be sure you are putting forth the strongest case for your client.

Make sure you have solid legal authority to back your argument.

You are entering a new professional community and learning a new intellectual discourse. Perfecting your legal writing is part of your training to prepare you to join that community.

Work hard, write well, and be happy.